PENGUIN PLAYS

JOHN BULL'S OTHER ISLAND

Bernard Shaw was born in Dublin in 1856. Essentially shy, he yet created the persona of G.B.S., the showman, satirist, controversialist, critic, pundit, wit, intellectual buffoon and dramatist. Commentators brought a new adjective into English: Shavian, a term used to embody all his brilliant qualities.

After his arrival in London in 1876 he became an active Socialist and a brilliant platform speaker. He wrote on many social aspects of the day; on *Commonsense about the War* (1914), *How to Settle the Irish Question* (1917) and *The Intelligent Woman's Guide to Socialism and Capitalism* (1928). He undertook his own education at the British Museum and consequently became keenly interested in cultural subjects. Thus his prolific output included music, art and theatre reviews, which were collected into several volumes, published as *Music in London 1890–1894* (3 vols., 1931); *Pen Portraits and Reviews* (1931); and *Our Theatres in the Nineties* (3 vols., 1931). Among his five novels, *Cashel Byron's Profession* and some shorter fiction including *The Black Girl in Search of God and Some Lesser Tales* are published in Penguins.

He conducted a strong attack on the London theatre and was closely associated with the intellectual revival of British theatre. His many plays fall into several categories: his 'Plays Unpleasant', 'Plays Pleasant', comedies, chronicle-plays, 'metabiological Pentateuch' (*Back to Methuselah*, a series of plays) and 'political extravaganzas'. G.B.S. died in 1950.

BERNARD SHAW

JOHN BULL'S
OTHER ISLAND

DEFINITIVE TEXT
under the editorial supervision of
Dan H. Laurence

PENGUIN BOOKS

Penguin Books Ltd, Harmondsworth, Middlesex, England
Viking Penguin Inc., 40 West 23rd Street, New York, New York 10010, U.S.A.
Penguin Books Australia Ltd, Ringwood, Victoria, Australia
Penguin Books Canada Ltd, 2801 John Street, Markham, Ontario, Canada L3R 1B4
Penguin Books (N.Z.) Ltd, 182–190 Wairau Road, Auckland 10, New Zealand

First published 1907
This revised text first published 1930
Published in Penguin Books 1984

Made and printed in Great Britain by
Cox and Wyman Ltd, Reading
Filmset in Monophoto Ehrhardt by
Northumberland Press Ltd, Gateshead

In Great Britain, all business connected with Bernard Shaw's plays is in the hands of THE SOCIETY OF AUTHORS, 84 Drayton Gardens, London SW10 9SD (Telephone: 01–373 6642), to which all inquiries and applications for licences should be addressed and fees paid. Dates and places of contemplated performances must be precisely stated in all applications.

In the United States of America and Canada, applications for permission to give stock and amateur performances of Bernard Shaw's plays should be made to Samuel French, Inc., 25 West 45th Street, New York, New York 10036. In all other cases, whether for stage, radio, or television, application should be made to the Society of Authors, 84 Drayton Gardens, London SW10 9SD, England.

Contents

Preface for Politicians

(written in 1906)

John Bull's Other Island was written in 1904 at the request of Mr William Butler Yeats, as a patriotic contribution to the repertory of the Irish Literary Theatre. Like most people who have asked me to write plays, Mr Yeats got rather more than he bargained for. The play was at that time beyond the resources of the new Abbey Theatre, which the Irish enterprise owed to the public spirit of Miss A. E. F. Horniman (an Englishwoman, of course), who, twelve years ago, played an important part in the history of the modern English stage as well as in my own personal destiny by providing the necessary capital for that memorable season at the Avenue Theatre which forced my Arms and The Man and Mr Yeats's Land of Heart's Desire on the recalcitrant London playgoer, and gave a third Irish playwright, Dr John Todhunter, an opportunity which the commercial theatres could not have afforded him.

There was another reason for changing the destination of John Bull's Other Island. It was uncongenial to the whole spirit of the neo-Gaelic movement, which is bent on creating a new Ireland after its own ideal, whereas my play is a very uncompromising presentment of the real old Ireland. The next thing that happened was the production of the play in London at the Court Theatre by Messrs Vedrenne and Barker, and its immediate and enormous popularity with delighted and flattered English audiences. This constituted it a successful commercial play, and made it unnecessary to resort to the special machinery or tax the special resources of the Irish Literary Theatre for its production.

HOW TOM BROADBENT TOOK IT

Now I have a good deal more to say about the relations between the Irish and the English than will be found in my play. Writing the play for an Irish audience, I thought it would be good for them to be shewn very clearly that the loudest laugh they could raise at the expense of the absurdest Englishman was not really a laugh on their side; that he would succeed where they would fail; that he could inspire strong affection and loyalty in an Irishman who knew the world and was moved only to dislike, mistrust, impatience and even exasperation by his own countrymen; that his power of taking himself seriously, and his insensibility to anything funny in danger and destruction, was the first condition of economy and concentration of force, sustained purpose, and rational conduct. But the need for this lesson in Ireland is the measure of its demoralizing superfluousness in England. English audiences very naturally swallowed it eagerly and smacked their lips over it, laughing all the more heartily because they felt that they were taking a caricature of themselves with the most tolerant and large-minded goodhumor. They were perfectly willing to allow me to represent Tom Broadbent as infatuated in politics, hypnotized by his newspaper leader-writers and parliamentary orators into an utter paralysis of his common sense, without moral delicacy or social tact, provided I made him cheerful, robust, goodnatured, free from envy, and above all, a successful muddler-through in business and love. Not only did no English critic allow that the success in business of Messrs English Broadbent and Irish Doyle might possibly have been due to some extent to Doyle, but one writer actually dwelt with much feeling on the pathos of Doyle's failure as an engineer (a circumstance not mentioned nor suggested in my play) in contrast with Broadbent's solid success. No doubt, when the play is performed in Ireland, the Dublin critics will regard it as self-evident that without Doyle Broadbent would have become bankrupt in six months. I should say, myself, that the combination was probably much more effective than either of the partners would have been alone. I am persuaded further – without pretending to know more about it than anyone else – that Broadbent's special contribution was simply the strength, self-satisfaction, social confidence and cheerful bumptiousness that money, comfort, and good feeding bring to all healthy people; and that Doyle's special contribution was the freedom from illusion, the power of facing facts, the nervous industry, the sharpened wits, the sensitive pride of the imaginative man who has fought his way up through social persecution and poverty. I do not say that the confidence of the Englishman in Broadbent is not for the moment justified. The virtues of the English soil are not less real because they consist of coal and iron, not of metaphysical sources of character. The virtues of Broadbent are not less real because they are the virtues of the money that coal and iron have produced. But as the mineral virtues are being discovered and developed in other soils, their derivative virtues are appearing so rapidly in other nations that Broadbent's relative advantage is vanishing. In truth I am afraid (the misgiving is natural to a by-this-time slightly elderly playwright) that Broadbent is out of date. The successful Englishman of today, when he is not a transplanted Scotchman or Irishman, often turns out on investigation to be, if not an American, an Italian, or a Jew, at least to be depending on the brains, the nervous energy, and the freedom from romantic illusions (often called cynicism) of such foreigners for the management of his sources of income. At all events I am persuaded that a modern nation that is satisfied with Broadbent is in a dream. Much as I like him, I object to be governed by him, or entangled in his political destiny. I therefore propose to give him a piece of my mind here, as an Irishman, full of an instinctive pity for those of my fellow-creatures who are only English.

WHAT IS AN IRISHMAN?

When I say that I am an Irishman I mean that I was born in Ireland, and that my native language is the English of Swift and not the unspeakable jargon of the mid-XIX century London newspapers. My extraction is the extraction of most Englishmen: that is, I have no trace in me of the commercially imported North Spanish strain which passes for aboriginal Irish: I am a genuine typical Irishman of the Danish, Norman, Cromwellian, and (of course) Scotch invasions. I am violently and arrogantly Protestant by family tradition; but let no English Government therefore count on my allegiance: I am English enough to be an inveterate Republican and Home Ruler. It is true that one of my grandfathers was an Orangeman; but then his sister was an abbess; and his uncle, I am proud to say, was hanged as a rebel. When I look round me on the hybrid cosmopolitans, slum poisoned or square pampered, who call themselves Englishmen today, and see them bullied by the Irish Protestant garrison as no Bengalee now lets himself be bullied by an Englishman; when I see the Irishman everywhere standing clearheaded, sane, hardily callous to the boyish sentimentalities, susceptibilities, and credulities that make the Englishman the dupe of every charlatan and the idolater of every numskull, I perceive that Ireland is the only spot on earth which still produces the ideal Englishman of history. Blackguard, bully, drunkard, liar, foulmouth, flatterer, beggar, backbiter, venal functionary, corrupt judge, envious friend, vindictive opponent, unparalleled political traitor: all these your Irishman may easily be, just as he may be a gentleman (a species extinct in England, and nobody a penny the worse); but he is never quite the hysterical, nonsense-crammed, fact-proof, truth-terrified, un-ballasted sport of all the bogey panics and all the silly enthusiasms that now calls itself 'God's Englishman'. England cannot do without its Irish and its Scots today, because it cannot do without at least a little sanity.

THE PROTESTANT GARRISON

The more Protestant an Irishman is – the more English he is, if it flatters you to have it put that way, the more intolerable he finds it to be ruled by English instead of Irish folly. A 'loyal' Irishman is an abhorrent phenomenon, because it is an unnatural one. No doubt English rule is vigorously exploited in the interests of the property, power, and promotion of the Irish classes as against the Irish masses. Our delicacy is part of a keen sense of reality which makes us a very practical, and even, on occasion, a very coarse people. The Irish soldier takes the King's shilling and drinks the King's health; and the Irish squire takes the title deeds of the English settlement and rises uncovered to the strains of the English national anthem. But do not mistake this cupboard loyalty for anything deeper. It gains a broad base from the normal attachment of every reasonable man to the established government as long as it is bearable; for we all, after a certain age, prefer peace to revolution and order to chaos, other things being equal. Such considerations produce loyal Irishmen as they produce loyal Poles and Fins, loyal Hindoos, loyal Filipinos, and faithful slaves. But there is nothing more in it than that. If there is an entire lack of gall in the feeling of the Irish gentry towards the English, it is because the Englishman is always gaping admiringly at the Irishman as at some clever child prodigy. He overrates him with a generosity born of a traditional conviction of his own superiority in the deeper aspects of human character. As the Irish gentleman, tracing his pedigree to the conquest or one of the invasions, is equally convinced that if this superiority really exists, he is the genuine true blue heir to it, and as he is easily able to hold his own in all the superficial social accomplishments, he finds English society agreeable, and English houses very comfortable, Irish establishments being generally straitened by an attempt to keep a park and a stable on an income which would not justify an Englishman in venturing upon a wholly detached villa.

OUR TEMPERAMENTS CONTRASTED

But however pleasant the relations between the Protestant garrison and the English gentry may be, they are always essentially of the nature of an *entente cordiale* between foreigners. Personally I like Englishmen much better than Irishmen (no doubt because they make more of me) just as many Englishmen like Frenchmen better than Englishmen, and never go on board a Peninsular and Oriental steamer when one of the ships of the Messageries Maritimes is available. But I never think of an Englishman as my countryman. I should as soon think of applying that term to a German. And the Englishman has the same feeling. When a Frenchman fails to make the distinction, we both feel a certain disparagement involved in the misapprehension. Macaulay, seeing that the Irish had in Swift an author worth stealing, tried to annex him by contending that he must be classed as an Englishman because he was not an aboriginal Celt. He might as well have refused the name of Briton to Addison because he did not stain himself blue and attach scythes to the poles of his sedan chair. In spite of all such trifling with facts, the actual distinction between the idolatrous Englishman and the fact-facing Irishman, of the same extraction though they be, remains to explode those two hollowest of fictions, the Irish and English 'races'. There is no Irish race any more than there is an English race or a Yankee race. There *is* an Irish climate, which will stamp an immigrant more deeply and durably in two years, apparently, than the English climate will in two hundred. It is reinforced by an artificial economic climate which does some of the work attributed to the natural geographic one; but the geographic climate is eternal and irresistible, making a mankind and a womankind that Kent, Middlesex, and East Anglia cannot produce and do not want to imitate.

How can I sketch the broad lines of the contrast as they strike me? Roughly I should say that the Englishman is wholly at the mercy of his imagination, having no sense of reality to check it. The Irishman, with a far subtler and more fastidious imagination, has one eye always on things

as they are. If you compare Moore's visionary Minstrel Boy with Mr
Rudyard Kipling's quasi-realistic Soldiers Three, you may yawn over
Moore or gush over him, but you will not suspect him of having had any
illusions about the contemporary British private; whilst as to Mr Kipling,
you will see that he has not, and unless he settles in Ireland for a few years
will always remain constitutionally and congenitally incapable of having,
the faintest inkling of the reality which he idolizes as Tommy Atkins.
Perhaps you have never thought of illustrating the contrast between
English and Irish by Moore and Mr Kipling, or even by Parnell and
Gladstone. Sir Boyle Roche and Shakespear may seem more to your point.
Let me find you a more dramatic instance. Think of the famous meeting
between the Duke of Wellington, that intensely Irish Irishman, and
Nelson, that intensely English Englishman. Wellington's contemptuous
disgust at Nelson's theatricality as a professed hero, patriot, and rhapsode,
a theatricality which in an Irishman would have been an insufferably
vulgar affectation, was quite natural and inevitable. Wellington's formula
for that kind of thing was a well-known Irish one: 'Sir: dont be a damned
fool.' It is the formula of all Irishmen for all Englishmen to this day. It is
the formula of Larry Doyle for Tom Broadbent in my play, in spite of
Doyle's affection for Tom. Nelson's genius, instead of producing intellectual keenness and scrupulousness, produced mere delirium. He was
drunk with glory, exalted by his fervent faith in the sound British
patriotism of the Almighty, nerved by the vulgarest anti-foreign prejudice,
and apparently unchastened by any reflections on the fact that he had
never had to fight a technically capable and properly equipped enemy
except on land, where he had never been successful. Compare Wellington,
who had to fight Napoleon's armies, Napoleon's marshals, and finally
Napoleon himself, without one moment of illusion as to the human
material he had to command, without one gush of the 'Kiss me, Hardy'
emotion which enabled Nelson to idolize his crews and his staff, without
forgetting even in his dreams that the normal British officer of that time
was an incapable amateur (as he still is) and the normal British soldier a
never-do-well (he is now a depressed and respectable young man). No
wonder Wellington became an accomplished comedian in the art of
anticlimax, scandalizing the unfortunate Croker, responding to the
demand for glorious sentiments by the most disenchanting touches of
realism, and, generally, pricking the English windbag at its most explosive

crises of distention. Nelson, intensely nervous and theatrical, made an enormous fuss about victories so cheap that he would have deserved shooting if he had lost them, and, not content with lavishing splendid fighting on helpless adversaries like the heroic De Brueys or Villeneuve (who had not even the illusion of heroism when he went like a lamb to the slaughter), got himself killed by his passion for exposing himself to death in that sublime defiance of it which was perhaps the supreme tribute of the exquisite coward to the King of Terrors (for, believe me, you cannot be a hero without being a coward: supersense cuts both ways), the result being a tremendous effect on the gallery. Wellington, most capable of captains, was neither a hero nor a patriot: perhaps not even a coward; and had it not been for the Nelsonic anecdotes invented for him – 'Up guards, and at em' and so forth – and the fact that the antagonist with whom he finally closed was such a master of theatrical effect that Wellington could not fight him without getting into his limelight, nor overthrow him (most unfortunately for us all) without drawing the eyes of the whole world to the catastrophe, the Iron Duke would have been almost forgotten by this time. Now that contrast is English against Irish all over, and is the more delicious because the real Irishman in it is the Englishman of tradition, whilst the real Englishman is the traditional theatrical foreigner.

The value of the illustration lies in the fact that Nelson and Wellington were both in the highest degree efficient, and both in the highest degree incompatible with one another on any other footing than one of independence. The government of Nelson by Wellington or of Wellington by Nelson is felt at once to be a dishonorable outrage to the governed and a finally impossible task for the governor.

I daresay some Englishman will now try to steal Wellington as Macaulay tried to steal Swift. And he may plead with some truth that though it seems impossible that any other country than England could produce a hero so utterly devoid of common sense, intellectual delicacy, and international chivalry as Nelson, it may be contended that Wellington was rather an eighteenth century aristocratic type, than a specifically Irish type. George IV and Byron, contrasted with Gladstone, seem Irish in respect of a certain humorous blackguardism, and a power of appreciating art and sentiment without being duped by them into mistaking romantic figments for realities. But faithlessness and the need for carrying off the worthlessness and impotence that accompany it, produce in all nations a gay, sceptical, amusing, blaspheming, witty fashion which suits the flexibility of the Irish mind very well; and the contrast between this fashion and the energetic infatuations that have enabled intellectually ridiculous men, without wit or humor, to go on crusades and make successful revolutions, must not be confused with the contrast between the English and Irish idiosyncrasies. The Irishman makes a distinction which the Englishman is too lazy intellectually (the intellectual laziness and slovenliness of the English is almost beyond belief) to make. The Englishman, impressed with the dissoluteness of the faithless wits of the Restoration and the Regency, and with the victories of the wilful zealots of the patriotic, religious, and revolutionary wars, jumps to the conclusion that wilfulness is the main thing. In this he is right. But he overdoes his jump so far as to conclude also that stupidity and wrong-headedness are better guarantees of efficiency and trustworthiness than intellectual vivacity, which he mistrusts as a common symptom of worthlessness, vice, and instability. Now in this he is most dangerously wrong. Whether the Irishman grasps the truth as firmly as the Englishman may be open to question; but he is certainly comparatively free from the error. That affectionate and admiring love of sentimental stupidity for its own sake, both in men and women, which shines so steadily through the novels of Thackeray would hardly be possible in the works of an Irish novelist. Even Dickens, though too vital a genius and too severely educated in the school of shabby-genteel poverty to have any doubt of the national danger of fatheadedness in high places, evidently assumes rather too hastily the superiority of Mr Meagles to Sir John Chester and Harold Skimpole. On the other hand, it takes an Irishman years of residence in England to learn to respect and like a blockhead. An Englishman will not respect nor like anyone else. Every English statesman has to maintain his popularity by pretending to be ruder, more ignorant, more sentimental, more super-stitious, more stupid than any man who has lived behind the scenes of public life for ten minutes can possibly be. Nobody dares to publish really intimate memoirs of him or really private letters of his until his whole generation has passed away, and his party can no longer be compromised by the discovery that the platitudinizing twaddler and hypocritical opportunist was really a man of some perception as well as of strong constitution, pegaway industry, personal ambition, and party keenness.

ENGLISH STUPIDITY EXCUSED

I do not claim it as a natural superiority in the Irish nation that it dislikes and mistrusts fools, and expects its political leaders to be clever and humbug-proof. It may be that if our resources included the armed force and virtually unlimited money which push the political and military figureheads of England through bungled enterprises to a muddled success, and create an illusion of some miraculous and divine innate English quality that enables a general to become a conqueror with abilities that would not suffice to save a cabman from having his license marked, and a member of parliament to become Prime Minister with the outlook on life of a sporting country solicitor educated by a private governess, we should lapse into gross intellectual sottishness, and prefer leaders who encouraged our vulgarities by sharing them, and flattered us by associating them with purchased successes, to our betters. But as it is, we cannot afford that sort of encouragement and flattery in Ireland. The odds against which our leaders have to fight would be too heavy for the fourth-rate Englishmen whose leadership consists for the most part in marking time ostentatiously until they are violently shoved, and then stumbling blindly forward (or backward) wherever the shove sends them. We cannot crush England as a Pickford's van might crush a perambulator. We are the perambulator and England the Pickford. We must study her and our real weaknesses and real strength; we must practise upon her slow conscience and her quick terrors; we must deal in ideas and political principles since we cannot deal in bayonets; we must outwit, outwork, outstay her; we must embarrass, bully, even conspire and assassinate when nothing else will move her, if we are not all to be driven deeper and deeper into the shame and misery of our servitude. Our leaders must be not only determined enough, but clever enough to do this. We have no illusions as to the existence of any mysterious Irish pluck, Irish honesty, Irish bias on the part of Providence, or sterling Irish solidity of character, that will enable an Irish blockhead to hold his own against England. Blockheads are of no use to us: we were compelled to follow a supercilious, unpopular, tongue-tied, aristocratic Protestant Parnell, although there was no lack among us of fluent imbeciles, with majestic presences and oceans of dignity and sentiment, to promote into his place could they have done his work for us. It is obviously convenient that Mr Redmond should be a better speaker and rhetorician than Parnell; but if he began to use his powers to make himself agreeable instead of making himself reckoned with by the enemy; if he set to work to manufacture and support English shams and hypocrisies instead of exposing and denouncing them; if he constituted himself the permanent apologist of doing nothing, and, when the people insisted on his doing something, only roused himself to discover how to pretend to do it without really changing anything, he would lose his leadership as certainly as an English politician would, by the same course, attain a permanent place on the front bench. In short, our circumstances place a premium on political ability whilst the circumstances of England discount it; and the quality of the supply naturally follows the demand. If you miss in my writings that hero-worship of dotards and duffers which is planting England with statues of disastrous statesmen and absurd generals, the explanation is simply that I am an Irishman and you an Englishman.

IRISH PROTESTANTISM REALLY PROTESTANT

When I repeat that I am an Irish Protestant, I come to a part of the relation between England and Ireland that you will never understand unless I insist on explaining it to you with that Irish insistence on intellectual clarity to which my English critics are so intensely recalcitrant.

First, let me tell you that in Ireland Protestantism is really Protestant. It is true that there is an Irish Protestant Church (disestablished some 35 years ago) in spite of the fact that a Protestant Church is, fundamentally, a contradiction in terms. But this means only that the Protestants use the word Church to denote their secular organization, without troubling themselves about the metaphysical sense of Christ's famous pun, 'Upon this rock I will build my church.' The Church of England, which is a reformed Anglican Catholic Anti-Protestant Church, is quite another affair. An Anglican is acutely conscious that he is not a Wesleyan; and many Anglican clergymen do not hesitate to teach that all Methodists incur damnation. In Ireland all that the member of the Irish Protestant Church knows is that he is not a Roman Catholic. The decorations of even the 'lowest' English Church seem to him to be extravagantly Ritualistic and Popish. I myself entered the Irish Church by baptism, a ceremony performed by my uncle in 'his own church'. But I was sent, with many boys of my own denomination, to a Wesleyan school where the Wesleyan catechism was taught without the least protest on the part of the parents, although there was so little presumption in favor of any boy there being a Wesleyan that if all the Church boys had been withdrawn at any moment, the school would have become bankrupt. And this was by no means analogous to the case of those working class members of the Church of England in London, who send their daughters to Roman Catholic schools rather than to the public elementary schools. They do so for the definite reason that the nuns teach girls good manners and sweetness of speech, which have no place in the County Council curriculum. But in Ireland the Church parent sends his son to a Wesleyan school (if it is convenient and socially eligible) because he is indifferent to the form of Protestantism provided it is Protestantism. There is also in Ireland a characteristically Protestant refusal to take ceremonies and even sacraments very seriously except by way of strenuous objection to them when they are conducted with candles or incense. For example, I was never confirmed, although the ceremony was specially needed in my case as the failure of my appointed godfather to appear at my baptism had led to his responsibilities being assumed on the spot, at my uncle's order, by the sexton. And my case was a very common one, even among people quite untouched by modern scepticisms. Apart from the weekly churchgoing, which holds its own as a respectable habit, the initiations are perfunctory, the omissions regarded as negligible. The distinction between churchman and dissenter, which in England is a class distinction, a political distinction, and even occasionally a religious distinction, does not exist. Nobody is surprised in Ireland to find that the squire who is the local pillar of the formerly established Church is also a Plymouth Brother, and, except on certain special or fashionable occasions, attends the Methodist meeting-house. The parson has no priestly character and no priestly influence: the High Church curate of course exists and has his vogue among religious epicures of the other sex; but the general attitude of his congregation towards him is that of Dr Clifford. The clause in the Apostles' creed professing belief in a Catholic Church is a standing puzzle to Protestant children; and when they grow up they dismiss it from their minds more often than they solve it, because they really are not Catholics but Protestants to the extremest practicable degree of individualism. It is true that they talk of church and chapel with all the Anglican contempt for chapel; but in Ireland the chapel means the Roman Catholic church, for which the Irish Protestant reserves all the class rancor, the political hostility, the religious bigotry, and the bad blood generally that in England separates the Establishment from the non-conforming Protestant organizations. When a vulgar Irish Protestant speaks of a 'Papist' he feels exactly as a vulgar Anglican vicar does when he speaks of a Dissenter. And when the vicar is Anglican enough to call himself a Catholic priest, wear a cassock, and bless his flock with two fingers, he becomes horrifically incomprehensible to the Irish Protestant Churchman, who, on his part, puzzles the Anglican by regarding a Methodist as tolerantly as an Irishman who likes grog regards an Irishman who prefers punch.

A FUNDAMENTAL ANOMALY

Now nothing can be more anomalous, and at bottom impossible, than a Conservative Protestant party standing for the established order against a revolutionary Catholic party. The Protestant is theoretically an anarchist as far as anarchism is practicable in human society: that is, he is an individualist, a freethinker, a self-helper, a Whig, a Liberal, a mistruster and vilifier of the State, a rebel. The Catholic is theoretically a Collectivist, a self-abnegator, a Tory, a Conservative, a supporter of Church and State one and undivisible, an obeyer. This would be a statement of fact as well as of theory if men were Protestants and Catholics by temperament and adult choice instead of by family tradition. The peasant who supposed that Wordsworth's son would carry on the business now the old gentleman was gone was not a whit more foolish than we who laugh at his ignorance of the nature of poetry whilst we take it as a matter of course that a son should 'carry on' his father's religion. Hence, owing to our family system, the Catholic Churches are recruited daily at the font by temperamental Protestants, and the Protestant organizations by temperamental Catholics, with consequences most disconcerting to those who expect history to be deducible from the religious professions of the men who make it.

Still, though the Roman Catholic Church may occasionally catch such Tartars as Luther and Voltaire, or the Protestant organizations as Newman and Manning, the general run of mankind takes its impress from the atmosphere in which it is brought up. In Ireland the Roman Catholic peasant cannot escape the religious atmosphere of his Church. Except when he breaks out like a naughty child he is docile; he is reverent; he is content to regard knowledge as something not his business; he is a child before his Church, and accepts it as the highest authority in science and philosophy. He speaks of himself as a son of the Church, calling his priest father instead of brother or Mister. To rebel politically, he must break away from tutelage and follow a Protestant leader on national questions. His Church naturally fosters his submissiveness. The British Government and the Vatican may differ very vehemently as to whose subject the Irishman is to be; but they are quite agreed as to the propriety of his being a subject. Of the two, the British Government allows him more liberty, giving him as complete a democratic control of local government as his means will enable him to use, and a voice in the election of a formidable minority in the House of Commons, besides allowing him to read and learn what he likes – except when it makes a tufthunting onslaught on a seditious newspaper. But if he dared to claim a voice in the selection of his parish priest, or a representative at the Vatican, he would be denounced from the altar as an almost inconceivable blasphemer; and his educational opportunities are so restricted by his Church that he is heavily handicapped in every walk of life that requires any literacy. It is the aim of his priest to make him and keep him a submissive Conservative; and nothing but gross economic oppression and religious persecution could have produced the strange phenomenon of a revolutionary movement not only tolerated by the Clericals, but, up to a certain point, even encouraged by them. If there is such a thing as political science, with natural laws like any other science, it is certain that only the most violent external force could effect and maintain this unnatural combination of political revolution with Papal reaction, and of hardy individualism and independence with despotism and subjugation.

That violent external force is the clumsy thumb of English rule. If you would be good enough, ladies and gentlemen of England, to take your thumb away and leave us free to do something else than bite it, the unnaturally combined elements in Irish politics would fly asunder and recombine according to their proper nature with results entirely satisfactory to real Protestantism.

THE NATURE OF POLITICAL HATRED

Just reconsider the Home Rule question in the light of that very English characteristic of the Irish people, their political hatred of priests. Do not be distracted by the shriek of indignant denial from the Catholic papers and from those who have witnessed the charming relations between the Irish peasantry and their spiritual fathers. I am perfectly aware that the Irish love their priests as devotedly as the French loved them before the Revolution or as the Italians loved them before they imprisoned the Pope in the Vatican. They love their landlords too: many an Irish gentleman has found in his nurse a foster-mother more interested in him than his actual mother. They love the English, as every Englishman who travels in Ireland can testify. Please do not suppose that I speak satirically: the world is full of authentic examples of the concurrence of human kindliness with political rancor. Slaves and schoolboys often love their masters; Napoleon and his soldiers made desperate efforts to save from drowning the Russian soldiers under whom they had broken the ice with their cannon; even the relations between nonconformist peasants and country parsons in England are not invariably unkindly; in the southern States of America planters are often traditionally fond of negroes and kind to them, with substantial returns in humble affection; soldiers and sailors often admire and cheer their officers sincerely and heartily; nowhere is actual personal intercourse found compatible for long with the intolerable friction of hatred and malice. But people who persist in pleading these amiabilities as political factors must be summarily bundled out of the room when questions of State are to be discussed. Just as an Irishman may have English friends whom he may prefer to any Irishman of his acquaintance, and be kind, hospitable, and serviceable in his intercourse with Englishmen, whilst being perfectly prepared to make the Shannon run red with English blood if Irish freedom could be obtained at that price; so an Irish Catholic may like his priest as a man and revere him as a confessor and spiritual pastor whilst being implacably determined to seize the first opportunity of throwing off his yoke. This is political hatred: the only hatred that civilization allows to be mortal hatred.

THE REVOLT AGAINST THE PRIEST

Realize, then, that the popular party in Ireland is seething with rebellion against the tyranny of the Church. Imagine the feelings of an English farmer if the parson refused to marry him for less than £20, and if he had virtually no other way of getting married! Imagine the Church Rates revived in the form of an unofficial Income Tax scientifically adjusted to your taxable capacity by an intimate knowledge of your affairs verified in the confessional! Imagine being one of a peasantry reputed the poorest in the world, under the thumb of a priesthood reputed the richest in the world! Imagine a Catholic middle class continually defeated in the struggle of professional, official, and fashionable life by the superior education of its Protestant competitors, and yet forbidden by its priests to resort to the only efficient universities in the country! Imagine trying to get a modern education in a seminary of priests, where every modern book worth reading is on the index, and the earth is still regarded, not perhaps as absolutely flat, yet as being far from so spherical as Protestants allege! Imagine being forbidden to read this preface because it proclaims your own grievance! And imagine being bound to submit to all this because the popular side must hold together at all costs in the face of the Protestant enemy! That is, roughly, the predicament of Roman Catholic Ireland.

PROTESTANT LOYALTY: A FORECAST

Now let us have a look at Protestant Ireland. I have already said that a 'loyal' Irishman is an abhorrent phenomenon, because he is an unnatural one. In Ireland it is not 'loyalty' to drink the English king's health and stand uncovered to the English national anthem: it is simply exploitation of English rule in the interests of the property, power, and promotion of the Irish classes as against the Irish masses. From any other point of view it is cowardice and dishonor. I have known a Protestant go to Dublin Castle to be sworn in as a special constable, quite resolved to take the baton and break the heads of a patriotic faction just then upsetting the peace of the town, yet back out at the last moment because he could not bring himself to swallow the oath of allegiance tendered with the baton. There is no such thing as genuine loyalty in Ireland. There is a separation of the Irish people into two hostile camps: one Protestant, gentlemanly, and oligarchical: the other Roman Catholic, popular, and democratic. The oligarchy governs Ireland as a bureaucracy deriving authority from the king of England. It cannot cast him off without casting off its own ascendancy. Therefore it naturally exploits him sedulously, drinking his health, waving his flag, playing his anthem, and using the foolish word 'traitor' freely in its cups. But let the English Government make a step towards the democratic party, and the Protestant garrison revolts at once, not with tears and prayers and anguish of soul and years of trembling reluctance, as the parliamentarians of the XVII century revolted against Charles I, but with acrid promptitude and strident threatenings. When England finally abandons the garrison by yielding to the demand for Home Rule, the Protestants will not go under, nor will they waste much time in sulking over their betrayal, and comparing their fate with that of Gordon left by Gladstone to perish on the spears of heathen fanatics. They cannot afford to retire into an Irish Faubourg St Germain. They will take an energetic part in the national government, which will be sorely in need of parliamentary and official forces independent of Rome. They will get not only the Protestant votes, but the votes of Catholics in that spirit of toleration which is everywhere extended to heresies that happen to be politically serviceable to the orthodox. They will not relax their determination to hold every inch of the government of Ireland that they can grasp; but as that government will then be a national Irish government instead of as now an English government, their determination will make them the vanguard of Irish Nationalism and Democracy as against Romanism and Sacerdotalism, leaving English Unionists grieved and shocked at their discovery of the true value of an Irish Protestant's loyalty.

But there will be no open break in the tradition of the party. The Protestants will still be the party of Union, which will then mean, not the repeal of Home Rule, but the maintenance of the Federal Union of English-speaking commonwealths, now theatrically called the Empire. They will pull down the Union Jack without the smallest scruple; but they know the value of the Channel Fleet, and will cling closer than brothers to that and any other Imperial asset that can be exploited for the protection of Ireland against foreign aggression or the sharing of expenses with the British taxpayer. They know that the Irish coast is for the English invasion-scaremonger the heel of Achilles, and that they can use this to make him pay for the boot.

PROTESTANT PUGNACITY

If any Englishman feels incredulous as to this view of Protestantism as an essentially Nationalist force in Ireland, let him ask himself which leader he, if he were an Irishman, would rather have back from the grave to fight England: the Catholic Daniel O'Connell or the Protestant Parnell. O'Connell organized the Nationalist movement only to draw its teeth, to break its determination, and to declare that Repeal of the Union was not worth the shedding of a drop of blood. He died in the bosom of his Church, not in the bosom of his country. The Protestant leaders, from Lord Edward Fitzgerald to Parnell, have never divided their devotion. If any Englishman thinks that they would have been more sparing of blood than the English themselves are, if only so cheap a fluid could have purchased the honor of Ireland, he greatly mistakes the Irish Protestant temper. The notion that Ireland is the only country in the world not worth shedding a drop of blood for is not a Protestant one, and certainly not countenanced by English practice. It was hardly reasonable to ask Parnell to shed blood *quant. suff.* in Egypt to put an end to the misgovernment of the Khedive and replace him by Lord Cromer for the sake of the English bondholders, and then to expect him to become a Tolstoyan or an O'Connellite in regard to his own country. With a wholly Protestant Ireland at his back he might have bullied England into conceding Home Rule; for the insensibility of the English governing classes to philosophical, moral, social considerations – in short, to any considerations which require a little intellectual exertion and sympathetic alertness – is tempered, as we Irish well know, by an absurd susceptibility to intimidation.

For let me halt a moment here to impress on you, O English reader, that no fact has been more deeply stamped into us than that we can do nothing with an English Government unless we frighten it, any more than you can yourself. When power and riches are thrown haphazard into children's cradles as they are in England, you get a governing class without industry, character, courage, or real experience; and under such circumstances reforms are produced only by catastrophes followed by panics in which 'something must be done'. Thus it costs a cholera epidemic to achieve a Public Health Act, a Crimean War to reform the Civil Service, and a gunpowder plot to disestablish the Irish Church. It was by the light, not of reason, but of the moon, that the need for paying serious attention to the Irish land question was seen in England. It cost the American War of Independence and the Irish Volunteer movement to obtain the Irish parliament of 1782, the constitution of which far overshot the nationalist mark of today in the matter of independence.

It is vain to plead that this is human nature and not class weakness. The Japanese have proved that it is possible to conduct social and political changes intelligently and providentially instead of drifting along helplessly until public disasters compel a terrified and inconsiderate rearrangement. Innumerable experiments in local government have shewn that when men are neither too poor to be honest nor too rich to understand and share the needs of the people – as in New Zealand, for example – they can govern much more providently than our little circle of aristocrats and plutocrats.

THE JUST ENGLISHMAN

English Unionists, when asked what they have to say in defence of their rule of subject peoples, often reply that the Englishman is just, leaving us divided between our derision of so monstrously inhuman a pretension, and our impatience with so gross a confusion of the mutually exclusive functions of judge and legislator. For there is only one condition on which a man can do justice between two litigants, and that is that he shall have no interest in common with either of them, whereas it is only by having every interest in common with both of them that he can govern them tolerably. The indispensable preliminary to Democracy is the representation of every interest: the indispensable preliminary to justice is the elimination of every interest. When we want an arbitrator or an umpire, we turn to a stranger: when we want a government, a stranger is the one person we will not endure. The Englishman in India, for example, stands, a very statue of justice, between two natives. He says, in effect, 'I am impartial in your religious disputes because I believe in neither of your religions. I am impartial in your conflicts of custom and sentiment because your customs and sentiments are different from, and abysmally inferior to, my own. Finally, I am impartial as to your interests because they are both equally opposed to mine, which is to keep you both equally powerless against me in order that I may extract money from you to pay salaries and pensions to my self and my fellow Englishmen as judges and rulers over you. In return for which you get the inestimable benefit of a government that does absolute justice as between Indian and Indian, being wholly preoccupied with the maintenance of absolute injustice as between India and England.'

It will be observed that no Englishman, without making himself ridiculous, could pretend to be perfectly just or disinterested in English affairs, or would tolerate a proposal to establish the Indian or Irish system in Great Britain. Yet if the justice of the Englishman is sufficient to ensure the welfare of India or Ireland, it ought to suffice equally for England. But the English are wise enough to refuse to trust to English justice themselves, preferring democracy. They can hardly blame the Irish for taking the same view.

In short, dear English reader, the Irish Protestant stands outside that English Mutual Admiration Society which you call the Union or the Empire. You may buy a common and not ineffective variety of Irish Protestant by delegating your powers to him, and in effect making him the oppressor and you his sorely bullied and bothered catspaw and military maintainer; but if you offer him nothing for his loyalty except the natural superiority of the English character, you will – well, try the experiment, and see what will happen! You would have a ten-times better chance with the Roman Catholic; for he has been saturated from his youth up with the Imperial idea of foreign rule by a spiritually superior international power, and is trained to submission and abnegation of his private judgment. A Roman Catholic garrison would take its orders from England and let her rule Ireland if England were Roman Catholic. The Protestant garrison simply seizes on the English power; uses it for its own purposes; and occasionally orders the English Government to remove an Irish secretary who has dared to apply English ideas to the affairs of the garrison. Whereupon the English Government abjectly removes him, and implores him, as a gentleman and a loyal Englishman, not to reproach it in the face of the Nationalist enemy.

Such incidents naturally do not shake the sturdy conviction of the Irish Protestant that he is more than a match for any English Government in determination and intelligence. Here, no doubt, he flatters himself; for his advantage is not really an advantage of character, but of comparative directness of interest, concentration of force on one narrow issue, simplicity of aim, with freedom from the scruples and responsibilities of world-politics. The business is Irish business, not English; and he is Irish. And his object, which is simply to secure the dominance of his own caste and creed behind the power of England, is simpler and clearer than the confused aims of English Cabinets struggling ineptly with the burdens of empire, and biassed by the pressure of capital anywhere rather than in Ireland. He has no responsibility, no interest, no status outside his own country and his own movement, which means that he has no conscience in dealing with England; whereas England, having a very uneasy conscience, and many hindering and hampering responsibilities and interests in dealing with him, gets bullied and driven by him, and finally learns sympathy with Nationalist aims by her experience of the tyranny of the Orange party.

IRISH CATHOLICISM FORECAST

Let us suppose that the establishment of a national government were to annihilate the oligarchic party by absorbing the Protestant garrison and making it a Protestant National Guard. The Roman Catholic laity, now a cipher, would organize itself; and a revolt against Rome and against the priesthood would ensue. The Roman Catholic Church would become the official Irish Church. The Irish parliament would insist on a voice in the promotion of churchmen; fees and contributions would be regulated; blackmail would be resisted; sweating in conventual factories and workshops would be stopped; and the ban would be taken off the universities. In a word, the Roman Catholic Church, against which Dublin Castle is powerless, would meet the one force on earth that can cope with it victoriously. That force is Democracy, a thing far more Catholic than itself. Until that force is let loose against it, the Protestant garrison can do nothing to the priesthood except consolidate it and drive the people to rally round it in defence of their altars against the foreigner and the heretic. When it *is* let loose, the Catholic laity will make as short work of sacerdotal tyranny in Ireland as it has done in France and Italy. And in doing so it will be forced to face the old problem of the relations of Church and State. A Roman Catholic party must submit to Rome: an anti-clerical Catholic party must of necessity become an Irish Catholic party. The Holy Roman Empire, like the other Empires, has no future except as a Federation of national Catholic Churches; for Christianity can no more escape Democracy than Democracy can escape Socialism. It is noteworthy in this connection that the Anglican Catholics have played and are playing a notable part in the Socialist movement in England in opposition to the individualist Secularists of the urban proletariat; but they are quit of the preliminary dead lift that awaits the Irish Catholic. Their Church has thrown off the yoke of Rome, and is safely and permanently Anglicized. But the Catholic Church in Ireland is still Roman. Home Rule will herald the day when the Vatican will go the way of Dublin Castle, and the island of the saints assume the headship of her own Church. It may seem incredible that long after the last Orangeman shall lay down his chalk for ever, the familiar scrawl on every blank wall in the north of Ireland 'To hell with the Pope!' may reappear in the south, traced by the hands of Catholics who shall have forgotten the traditional counter legend, 'To hell with King William!' (of glorious, pious, and immortal memory); but it may happen so. 'The island of the saints' is no idle phrase. Religious genius is one of our national products; and Ireland is no bad rock to build a Church on. Holy and beautiful is the soul of Catholic Ireland: her prayers are lovelier than the teeth and claws of Protestantism, but not so effective in dealing with the English.

ENGLISH VOLTAIREANISM

Let me familiarize the situation by shewing how closely it reproduces the English situation in its essentials. In England, as in France, the struggle between the priesthood and the laity has produced a vast body of Voltaireans. But the essential identity of the French and English movements has been obscured by the ignorance of the ordinary Englishman, who, instead of knowing the distinctive tenets of his church or sect, vaguely believes them to be the eternal truth as opposed to the damnable error of all the other denominations. He thinks of Voltaire as a French 'infidel', instead of as the champion of the laity against the official theocracy of the State Church. The Nonconformist leaders of our Free Churches are all Voltaireans. The warcry of the Passive Resisters is Voltaire's warcry, 'Écrasez l'infâme.' No account need be taken of the technical difference between Voltaire's 'infâme' and Dr Clifford's. One was the unreformed Roman Church of France; the other is the reformed Anglican Church; but in both cases the attack has been on a priestly tyranny and a professional monopoly. Voltaire convinced the Genevan ministers that he was the philosophic champion of their Protestant, Individualistic, Democratic Deism against the State Church of Roman Catholic France; and his heroic energy and beneficence as a philanthropist, which now only makes the list of achievements on his monument at Ferney the most impressive epitaph in Europe, then made the most earnest of the Lutheran ministers glad to claim a common inspiration with him. Unfortunately Voltaire had an irrepressible sense of humor. He joked about Habakkuk; and jokes about Habakkuk smelt too strongly of brimstone to be tolerated by Protestants to whom the Bible was not a literature but a fetish and a talisman. And so Voltaire, in spite of the church he 'erected to God', became in England the bogey-atheist of three generations of English ignoramuses, instead of the legitimate successor of Martin Luther and John Knox.

Nowadays, however, Voltaire's jokes are either forgotten or else fall flat on a world which no longer venerates Habakkuk; and his true position is becoming apparent. The fact that Voltaire was a Roman Catholic layman, educated at a Jesuit college, is the conclusive reply to the shallow people who imagine that Ireland delivered up to the Irish democracy – that is, to the Catholic laity – would be delivered up to the tyranny of the priesthood.

SUPPOSE!

Suppose, now, that the conquest of France by Henry V of England had endured, and that France in the XVIII century had been governed by an English viceroy through a Huguenot bureaucracy and a judicial bench appointed on the understanding that loyalty for them meant loyalty to England, and patriotism a willingness to die in defence of the English conquest and of the English Church, would not Voltaire in that case have been the meanest of traitors and self-seekers if he had played the game of England by joining in its campaign against his own and his country's Church? The energy he threw into the defence of Calas and Sirven would have been thrown into the defence of the Frenchmen whom the English would have called 'rebels'; and he would have been forced to identify the cause of freedom and democracy with the cause of 'l'infâme'. The French revolution would have been a revolution against England and English rule instead of against aristocracy and ecclesiasticism; and all the intellectual and spiritual forces in France, from Turgot to De Tocqueville, would have been burnt up in mere anti-Anglicism and nationalist dithyrambs instead of contributing to political science and broadening the thought of the world.

What would have happened in France is what has happened in Ireland; and that is why it is only the small-minded Irish, incapable of conceiving what religious freedom means to a country, who do not loathe English rule. For in Ireland England is nothing but the Pope's policeman. She imagines she is holding the Vatican cardinals at bay when she is really strangling the Voltaires, the Foxes and Penns, the Cliffords, Hortons, Campbells, Walters, and Silvester Hornes, who are to be found among the Roman Catholic laity as plentifully as among the Anglican Catholic laity in England. She gets nothing out of Ireland but infinite trouble, infinite confusion and hindrance in her own legislation, a hatred that circulates through the whole world and poisons it against her, a reproach that makes her professions of sympathy with Finland and Macedonia ridiculous and hypocritical, whilst the priest takes all the spoils, in money, in power, in pride, and in popularity.

IRELAND'S REAL GRIEVANCE

But it is not the spoils that matter. It is the waste, the sterilization, the perversion of fruitful brain power into flatulent protest against unnecessary evil, the use of our very entrails to tie our own hands and seal our own lips in the name of our honor and patriotism. As far as money or comfort is concerned, the average Irishman has a more tolerable life – especially now that the population is so scanty – than the average Englishman. It is true that in Ireland the poor man is robbed and starved and oppressed under judicial forms which confer the imposing title of justice on a crude system of bludgeoning and perjury. But so is the Englishman. The Englishman, more docile, less dangerous, too lazy intellectually to use such political and legal power as lies within his reach, suffers more and makes less fuss about it than the Irishman. But at least he has nobody to blame but himself and his fellow countrymen. He does not doubt that if an effective majority of the English people made up their minds to alter the Constitution, as the majority of the Irish people have made up their minds to obtain Home Rule, they could alter it without having to fight an overwhelmingly powerful and rich neighboring nation, and fight, too, with ropes round their necks. He can attack any institution in his country without betraying it to foreign vengeance and foreign oppression. True, his landlord may turn him out of his cottage if he goes to a Methodist chapel instead of to the parish church. His customers may stop their orders if he votes Liberal instead of Conservative. English ladies and gentlemen who would perish sooner than shoot a fox do these things without the smallest sense of indecency and dishonor. But they cannot muzzle his intellectual leaders. The English philosopher, the English author, the English orator can attack every abuse and expose every supersitition without strengthening the hands of any common enemy. In Ireland every such attack, every such exposure, is a service to England and a stab to Ireland. If you expose the tyranny and rapacity of the Church, it is an argument in favor of Protestant ascendency. If you denounce the nepotism and jobbery of the new local authorities, you are demonstrating the unfitness of the Irish to govern themselves, and the superiority of the old oligarchical grand juries.

And there is the same pressure on the other side. The Protestant must stand by the garrison at all costs: the Unionist must wink at every bureaucratic abuse, connive at every tyranny, magnify every official blockhead, because their exposure would be a victory for the Nationalist enemy. Every Irishman is in Lancelot's position: his honor rooted in dishonor stands; and faith unfaithful keeps him falsely true.

THE CURSE OF NATIONALISM

It is hardly possible for an Englishman to understand all that this implies. A conquered nation is like a man with cancer: he can think of nothing else, and is forced to place himself, to the exclusion of all better company, in the hands of quacks who profess to treat or cure cancer. The windbags of the two rival platforms are the most insufferable of all windbags. It requires neither knowledge, character, conscience, diligence in public affairs, nor any virtue, private or communal, to thump the Nationalist or Orange tub: nay, it puts a premium on the rancor or callousness that has given rise to the proverb that if you put an Irishman on a spit you can always get another Irishman to baste him. Jingo oratory in England is sickening enough to serious people: indeed one evening's mafficking in London produced a determined call for the police. Well, in Ireland all political oratory is Jingo oratory; and all political demonstrations are maffickings. English rule is such an intolerable abomination that no other subject can reach the people. Nationalism stands between Ireland and the light of the world. Nobody in Ireland of any intelligence likes Nationalism any more than a man with a broken arm likes having it set. A healthy nation is as unconscious of its nationality as a healthy man of his bones. But if you break a nation's nationality it will think of nothing else but getting it set again. It will listen to no reformer, to no philosopher, to no preacher, until the demand of the Nationalist is granted. It will attend to no business, however vital, except the business of unification and liberation.

That is why everything is in abeyance in Ireland pending the achievement of Home Rule. The great movements of the human spirit which sweep in waves over Europe are stopped on the Irish coast by the English guns of the Pigeon House Fort. Only a quaint little offshoot of English pre-Raphaelitism called the Gaelic movement has got a footing by using Nationalism as a stalking-horse, and popularizing itself as an attack on the native language of the Irish people, which is most fortunately also the native language of half the world, including England. Every election is fought on nationalist grounds; every appointment is made on nationalist grounds; every judge is a partisan in the nationalist conflict; every speech is a dreary recapitulation of nationalist twaddle; every lecture is a corruption of history to flatter nationalism or defame it; every school is a recruiting station; every church is a barrack; and every Irishman is unspeakably tired of the whole miserable business, which nevertheless is and perforce must remain his first business until Home Rule makes an end of it, and sweeps the nationalist and the garrison hack together into the dustbin.

There is indeed no greater curse to a nation than a nationalist movement, which is only the agonizing symptom of a suppressed natural function. Conquered nations lose their place in the world's march because they can do nothing but strive to get rid of their nationalist movements by recovering their national liberty. All demonstrations of the virtues of a foreign government, though often conclusive, are as useless as demonstrations of the superiority of artificial teeth, glass eyes, silver windpipes, and patent wooden legs to the natural products. Like Democracy, national self-government is not for the good of the people: it is for the satisfaction of the people. One Antonine emperor, one St Louis, one Richelieu, may be worth ten democracies in point of what is called good government; but there is no satisfaction for the people in them. To deprive a dyspeptic of his dinner and hand it over to a man who can digest it better is a highly logical proceeding; but it is not a sensible one. To take the government of Ireland away from the Irish and hand it over to the English on the ground that they can govern better would be a precisely parallel case if the English had managed their own affairs so well as to place their superior faculty for governing beyond question. But as the English are avowed muddlers – rather proud of it, in fact – even the logic of that case against Home Rule is not complete. Read Mr Charles Booth's account of London, Mr Rowntree's account of York, and the latest official report on Dundee; and then pretend, if you can, that Englishmen and Scotchmen have not more cause to hand over their affairs to an Irish parliament than to clamor for another nation's cities to devastate and another people's business to mismanage.

A NATURAL RIGHT

The question is not one of logic at all, but of natural right. English universities have for some time past encouraged an extremely foolish academic exercise which consists in disproving the existence of natural rights on the ground that they cannot be deduced from the principles of any known political system. If they could, they would not be natural rights but acquired ones. Acquired rights are deduced from political constitutions; but political constitutions are deduced from natural rights. When a man insists on certain liberties without the slightest regard to demonstrations that they are not for his own good, nor for the public good, nor moral, nor reasonable, nor decent, nor compatible with the existing constitution of society, then he is said to claim a natural right to that liberty. When, for instance, he insists on living, in spite of the irrefutable demonstrations of many able pessimists, from the author of the book of Ecclesiastes to Schopenhauer, that life is an evil, he is asserting a natural right to live. When he insists on a vote in order that his country may be governed according to his ignorance instead of the wisdom of the Privy Council, he is asserting a natural right to self-government. When he insists on guiding himself at 21 by his own inexperience and folly and immaturity instead of by the experience and sagacity of his father, or the well-stored mind of his grandmother, he is asserting a natural right to independence. Even if Home Rule was as unhealthy as an Englishman's eating, as intemperate as his drinking, as filthy as his smoking, as licentious as his domesticity, as corrupt as his elections, as murderously greedy as his commerce, as cruel as his prisons, and as merciless as his streets, Ireland's claim to self-government would still be as good as England's. King James the First proved so cleverly and conclusively that the satisfaction of natural rights was incompatible with good government that his courtiers called him Solomon. We, more enlightened, call him Fool, solely because we have learnt that nations insist on being governed by their own consent – or, as they put it, by themselves and for themselves – and that they will finally upset a good government which denies them this even if the alternative be a bad government which at least creates and maintains an illusion of democracy. America, as far as one can ascertain, is much worse governed, and has a much more disgraceful political history than England under Charles I; but the American Republic is the stabler government because it starts from a formal concession of natural rights, and keeps up an illusion of safeguarding them by an elaborate machinery of democratic election. And the final reason why Ireland must have Home Rule is that she has a natural right to it.

A WARNING

Finally, some words of warning to both nations. Ireland has been deliberately ruined again and again by England. Unable to compete with us industrially, she has destroyed our industries by the brute force of prohibitive taxation. She was perfectly right. That brute force was a more honorable weapon than the poverty which we used to undersell her. We lived with and as our pigs, and let loose our wares in the Englishman's market at prices which he could compete with only by living like a pig himself. Having the alternative of stopping our industry altogether, he very naturally and properly availed himself of it. We should have done the same in his place. To bear malice against him on that score is to poison our blood and weaken our constitutions with unintelligent rancor. In wrecking all the industries that were based on the poverty of our people England did us an enormous service. In omitting to do the same on her own soil, she did herself a wrong that has rotted her almost to the marrow. I hope that when Home Rule is at last achieved, one of our first legislative acts will be to fortify the subsistence of our people behind the bulwark of a standard wage, and to impose crushing import duties on every English trade that flourishes in the slum and fattens on the starvation of our unfortunate English neighbors.

DOWN WITH THE SOLDIER!

Now for England's share of warning. Let her look to her Empire; for unless she makes it such a Federation for civil strength and defence that all free peoples will cling to it voluntarily, it will inevitably become a military tyranny to prevent them from abandoning it; and such a tyranny will drain the English taxpayer of his money more effectually than its worst cruelties can ever drain its victims of their liberty. A political scheme that cannot be carried out except by soldiers will not be a permanent one. The soldier is an an anachronism of which we must get rid. Among people who are proof against the suggestions of romantic fiction there can no longer be any question of the fact that military service produces moral imbecility, ferocity, and cowardice, and that the defence of nations must be undertaken by the civil enterprise of men enjoying all the rights and liberties of citizenship, and trained by the exacting discipline of democratic freedom and responsibility. For permanent work the soldier is worse than useless: such efficiency as he has is the result of dehumanization and disablement. His whole training tends to make him a weakling. He has the easiest of lives: he has no freedom and no responsibility. He is politically and socially a child, with rations instead of rights, treated like a child, punished like a child, dressed prettily and washed and combed like a child, excused for outbreaks of naughtiness like a child, forbidden to marry like a child, and called Tommy like a child. He has no real work to keep him from going mad except housemaid's work: all the rest is forced exercise, in the form of endless rehearsals for a destructive and terrifying performance which may never come off, and which, when it does come off, is not like the rehearsals. His officer has not even housekeeper's work to keep him sane. The work of organizing and commanding bodies of men, which builds up the character and resource of the large class of civilians who live by it, only demoralizes the military officer, because his orders, however disastrous or offensive, must be obeyed without regard to consequences: for instance, if he calls his men dogs, and perverts a musketry drill order to make them kneel to him as an act of personal humiliation, and thereby provokes a mutiny among men not yet thoroughly broken in to the abjectness of the military condition, he is not, as might be expected, shot, but, at worst, reprimanded, whilst the leader of the mutiny, instead of getting the Victoria Cross and a public testimonial, is condemned to five years' penal servitude by Lynch Law (technically called martial law) administered by a trade union of officers. Compare with this the position of, for instance, our railway managers or our heads of explosive factories. They have to handle large bodies of men whose carelessness or insubordination may cause wholesale destruction of life and property; yet any of these men may insult them, defy them, or assault them without special penalties of any sort. The military commander dares not face these conditions: he lives in perpetual terror of his men, and will undertake their command only when they are stripped of all their civil rights, gagged, and bound hand and foot by a barbarous slave code. Thus the officer learns to punish, but never to rule; and when an emergency like the Indian Mutiny comes, he breaks down; and the situation has to be saved by a few untypical officers with character enough to have retained their civilian qualities in spite of the messroom. This, unfortunately, is learnt by the public, not on the spot, but from Lord Roberts fifty years later.

Besides the Mutiny we have had the Crimean and South African wars, the Dreyfus affair in France, the incidents of the anti-militarist campaign by the Social-Democrats in Germany, and now the Denshawai affair in the Nile delta, all heaping on us sensational demonstrations of the fact that soldiers pay the penalty of their slavery and outlawry by becoming, relatively to free civilians, destructive, cruel, dishonest, tyrannical, hysterical, mendacious, alarmists at home and terrorists abroad, politically reactionary, and professionally incapable. If it were humanly possible to militarize all the humanity out of a man, there would be absolutely no defence to this indictment. But the military system is so idiotically academic and impossible, and renders its victims so incapable of carrying it out with any thoroughness except when, in an occasional hysterical outburst of terror and violence, that hackneyed comedy of civil life, the weak man putting his foot down, becomes the military tragedy of the armed man burning, flogging, and murdering in a panic, that a body of soldiers and officers is in the main, and under normal circumstances, much like any other body of laborers and gentlemen. Many of us count among our personal friends and relatives officers whose amiable and honorable character seems to contradict everything I have just said about the military character. You have only to describe Lynch courts and acts of terrorism to them as the work of Ribbonmen, Dacoits, Moonlighters, Boxers, or – to use the general term most familiar to them – 'natives', and their honest and generous indignation knows no bounds: they feel about them like men, not like soldiers. But the moment you bring the professional side of them uppermost by describing precisely the same proceedings to them as the work of regular armies, they defend them, applaud them, and are ready to take part in them as if their humanity had been blown out like a candle. You find that there is a blind spot on their moral retina, and that this blind spot is the military spot.

The excuse, when any excuse is made, is that discipline is supremely important in war. Now most soldiers have no experience of war; and to assume that those who have are therefore qualified to legislate for it, is as absurd as to assume that a man who has been run over by an omnibus is thereby qualified to draw up wise regulations for the traffic of London. Neither our military novices nor our veterans are clever enough to see that in the field, discipline either keeps itself or goes to pieces; for humanity under fire is a quite different thing from humanity in barracks: when there is danger the difficulty is never to find men who will obey, but men who can command. It is in time of peace, when an army is either a police force (in which case its work can be better done by a civilian constabulary) or an absurdity, that discipline is difficult, because the wasted life of the soldier is unnatural, except to a lazy man, and his servitude galling and senseless, except to a docile one. Still, the soldier is a man, and the officer sometimes a gentleman in the literal sense of the word; and so, what with humanity, laziness, and docility combined, they manage to rub along with only occasional outbursts of mutiny on the one side and class rancor and class cowardice on the other.

They are not even discontented; for the military and naval codes simplify life for them just as it is simplified for children. No soldier is asked to think for himself, to judge for himself, to consult his own honor and manhood, to dread any consequence except the consequence of punishment to his own person. The rules are plain and simple; the ceremonies of respect and submission are as easy and mechanical as a prayer wheel; the orders are always to be obeyed thoughtlessly, however inept or dishonorable they may be. As the late Laureate said in the two stinging lines in which he branded the British soldier with the dishonor of Esau, 'theirs not to reason why, theirs but to do and die.' To the moral imbecile and political sluggard these conditions are as congenial and attractive as they are abhorrent and intolerable to the William Tell temperament. Just as the most incorrigible criminal is always, we are told, the best behaved convict, so the man with least conscience and initiative makes the best behaved soldier, and that not wholly through mere fear of punishment, but through a genuine fitness for and consequent happiness in the child-like military life. Such men dread freedom and responsibility as a weak man dreads a risk or a heavy burden; and the objection to the military system is that it tends to produce such men by a weakening disuse of the moral muscles. No doubt this weakness is just what the military system aims at, its ideal soldier being, not a complete man, but a docile unit of cannon-fodder which can be trusted to respond promptly and certainly to the external stimulus of a shouted order, and is intimidated to the pitch of being afraid to run away from a battle. It may be doubted whether even in the Prussian heyday of the system, when floggings of hundreds and even thousands of lashes were matters of ordinary routine, this detestable ideal was ever realized; but your courts-martial are not practical enough to take that into account: it is characteristic of the military mind continually to ignore human nature and cry for the moon instead of facing modern social facts and accepting modern democratic conditions. And when I say the military mind, I repeat that I am not forgetting the patent fact that the military mind and the humane mind can exist in the same person; so that an officer who will take all the civilian risks, from city traffic to foxhunting, without uneasiness, and who will manage all the civil employees on his estate and in his house and stables without the aid of a Mutiny Act, will also, in his military capacity, frantically declare that he dare not walk about in a foreign country unless every crime of violence against an Englishman in uniform is punished by the bombardment and destruction of a whole village, or the wholesale flogging and execution of every native in the neighborhood, and also that unless he and his fellow-officers have power, without the intervention of a jury, to punish the slightest self-assertion or hesitation to obey orders, however grossly insulting or disastrous those orders may be, with sentences which are reserved in civil life for the worst crimes, he cannot secure the obedience and respect of his men, and the country will accordingly lose all its colonies and dependencies, and be helplessly conquered in the German invasion which he confidently expects to occur in the course of a fortnight or so. That is to say, in so far as he is an ordinary gentleman he behaves sensibly and courageously; and in so far as he is a military man he gives way without shame to the grossest folly, cruelty and poltroonery. If any other profession in the world had been stained by these vices, and by false witness, forgery, swindling, torture, compulsion of men's families to attend their executions, digging up and mutilation of dead enemies, all wantonly added to the devastation proper to its own business, as the military profession has been within recent memory in England, France, and the United States of America (to mention no other countries), it would be very difficult to induce men of capacity and character to enter it. And in England it is, in fact, largely dependent for its recruits on the refuse of industrial life, and for its officers on the aristocratic and plutocratic refuse of political and diplomatic life, who join the army and pay for their positions in the more or less fashionable clubs which the regimental messes provide them with – clubs which, by the way, occasionally figure in ragging scandals as circles of extremely coarse moral character.

Now in countries which are denied Home Rule: that is, in which the government does not rest on the consent of the people, it must rest on military coercion; and the bureaucracy, however civil and legal it may be in form and even in the character of its best officials, must connive at all the atrocities of military rule, and become infected in the end with the chronic panic characteristic of militarism. In recent witness whereof, let me shift the scene from Ireland to Egypt, and tell the story of the Denshawai affair of June 1906 by way of object-lesson.

THE DENSHAWAI HORROR

Denshawai is a little Egyptian village in the Nile delta. Besides the dilapidated huts among the reeds by the roadside, and the palm trees, there are towers of unbaked brick, as unaccountable to an English villager as a Kentish oast-house to an Egyptian. These towers are pigeon-houses; for the villagers keep pigeons just as an English farmer keeps poultry.

Try to imagine the feelings of an English village if a party of Chinese officers suddenly appeared and began shooting the ducks, the geese, the hens, and the turkeys, and carried them off, asserting that they were wild birds, as everybody in China knew, and that the pretended indignation of the farmers was a cloak for hatred of the Chinese, and perhaps for a plot to overthrow the religion of Confucius and establish the Church of England in its place! Well, that is the British equivalent of what happened at Denshawai when a party of English officers went pigeon-shooting there the year before last. The inhabitants complained and memorialized; but they obtained no redress: the law failed them in their hour of need. So one leading family of pigeon farmers, Mahfouz by name, despaired of the law; and its head, Hassan Mahfouz, aged 60, made up his mind not to submit tamely to a repetition of the outrage. Also, British officers were ordered not to shoot pigeons in the villages without the consent of the Omdeh, or headman, though nothing was settled as to what might happen to the Omdeh if he ventured to refuse.

Fancy the feelings of Denshawai when on the 13th of June last there drove to the village four khaki-clad British officers with guns, one of them being a shooter of the year before, accompanied by one other officer on horseback, and also by a dragoman and an Ombashi, or police official! The oriental blood of Hassan Mahfouz boiled; and he warned them that they would not be allowed to shoot pigeons; but as they did not understand his language, the warning had no effect. They sent their dragoman to ask the Omdeh's permission to shoot; but the Omdeh was away; and all the interpreter could get from the Omdeh's deputy, who knew better than to dare an absolute refusal, was the pretty obvious reply that they might shoot if they went far enough away from the village. On the strength of this welcome, they went from 100 to 300 yards away from the houses (these distances were afterwards officially averaged at 500 yards), and began shooting the villagers' pigeons. The villagers remonstrated and finally seized the gun of the youngest officer. It went off in the struggle, and wounded three men and the wife of one Abd-el-Nebi, a young man of 25. Now the lady, though, as it turned out, only temporarily disabled by a charge of pigeon shot in the softest part of her person, gave herself up for dead; and the feeling in the village was much as if our imaginary Chinese officers, on being interfered with in their slaughter of turkeys, had killed an English farmer's wife. Abd-el-Nebi, her husband, took the matter to heart, not altogether without reason, we may admit. His threshing-floor also caught fire somehow (the official English theory is that he set it on fire as a signal for revolt to the entire Moslem world); and all the lads and loafers in the place were presently on the spot. The other officers, seeing their friend in trouble, joined him. Abd-el-Nebi hit the supposed murderer of his wife with a stick; Hassan Mahfouz used a stick also; and the lads and loafers began to throw stones and bricks. Five London policemen would have seen that there was nothing to be done but fight their way out, as there is no use arguing with an irritated mob, especially if you do not know its language. Had the shooting party been in the charge of a capable non-commissioned officer, he would perhaps have got it safely off. As it was, the officers tried propitiation, making their overtures in pantomime. They gave up their guns; they offered watches and money to the crowd, crying Baksheesh; and the senior officer actually collared the junior and pretended to arrest him for the murder of the woman. Naturally they were mobbed worse than before; and what they did not give to the crowd was taken from them, whether as payment for the pigeons, blood money, or simple plunder was not gone into. The officers, two Irishmen and three Englishmen, having made a hopeless mess of it, and being now in serious danger, made for their carriages, but were dragged out of them again, one of the coachmen being knocked senseless. They then 'agreed to run', the arrangement being that the Englishmen, being the juniors, should run away to camp and bring help to the Irishmen. They bolted accordingly; but the third, the youngest, seeing the two Irishmen hard put to it, went back and stood by them. Of the two fugitives, one, after a long race in the Egyptian afternoon sun, got to the next village and there dropped, smitten by sunstroke, of which he died. The other ran on and met a patrol, which started to the rescue.

Meanwhile, the other three officers had been taken out of the hands of the lads and the loafers, of Abd-el-Nebi and Hassan Mahfouz, by the elders and watchmen, and saved from further injury, but not before they had been severely knocked about, one of them having one of the bones of his left arm broken near the wrist – simple fracture of the thin end of the ulna. They were also brought to the threshing-floor; shewn the wounded woman; informed by gestures that they deserved to have their throats cut for murdering her; and kicked (with naked feet, fortunately); but at this point the elders and constables stopped the mobbing. Finally the three were sent off to camp in their carriages; and the incident ended for that day.

No English mob, under similar provocation, would have behaved any better; and few would have done as little mischief. It is not many months since an old man – not a foreigner and not an unbeliever – was kicked to death in the streets of London because the action of a park constable in turning him out of a public park exposed him to suspicion of misconduct. At Denshawai, the officers were not on duty. In their private capacity as sportsmen, they committed a serious depredation on a very poor village by slaughtering its stock. In an English village they would have been tolerated because the farmers would have expected compensation for damage, and the villagers coals and blankets and employment in country house, garden and stable, or as beaters, huntsmen and the like, from them. But Denshawai had no such inducements to submit to their thoughtless and selfish aggression. One of them had apparently killed a woman and wounded three men with his gun: in fact his own comrade virtually convicted him of it before the crowd by collaring him as a prisoner. In short, the officers had given outrageous provocation; and they had shewn an amiable but disastrous want of determination and judgment in dealing with the riot they provoked. They should have been severely reprimanded and informed that they had themselves to thank for what happened to them; and the villagers who assaulted them should have been treated with leniency, and assured that pigeon-shooting would not be allowed in future.

That is what should have ensued. Now for what actually did ensue.

Abd-el-Nebi, in consideration of the injury to his wife, was only sentenced to penal servitude for life. And our clemency did not stop there. His wife was not punished at all – not even charged with stealing the shot which was found in her person. And lest Abd-el-Nebi should feel lonely at 25 in beginning penal servitude for the rest of his days, another young man, of 20, was sent to penal servitude for life with him.

No such sentimentality was shewn to Hassan Mahfouz. An Egyptian pigeon farmer who objects to Brtish sport; threatens British officers and gentlemen when they shoot his pigeons; and actually hits those officers with a substantial stick, is clearly a ruffian to be made an example of. Penal servitude was not enough for a man of 60 who looked 70, and might not have lived to suffer five years of it. So Hassan was hanged; but as a special mark of consideration for his family, he was hanged in full view of his own house, with his wives and children and grandchildren enjoying the spectacle from the roof. And lest this privilege should excite jealousy in other households, three other Denshavians were hanged with him. They went through the ceremony with dignity, professing their faith ('Mahometan, I regret to say,' Mr Pecksniff would have said). Hassan, however, 'in a loud voice invoked ruin upon the houses of those who had given evidence against him'; and Darweesh was impatient and presumed to tell the hangman to be quick. But then Darweesh was a bit of a brigand: he had been imprisoned for bearing false witness; and his resistance to the British invasion is the only officially recorded incident of his life which is entirely to his credit. He and Abd-el-Nebi (who had been imprisoned for theft) were the only disreputable characters among the punished. Ages of the four hanged men respectively, 60, 50, 22 and 20.

Hanging, however, is the least sensational form of public execution: it lacks those elements of blood and torture for which the military and bureaucratic imagination lusts. So, as they had room for only one man on the gallows, and had to leave him hanging half an hour to make sure work and give his family plenty of time to watch him swinging ('slowly turning round and round on himself', as the local papers described it), thus having two hours to kill as well as four men, they kept the entertainment going by flogging eight men with fifty lashes each: eleven more than the utmost permitted by the law of Moses in times which our Army of Occupation no doubt considers barbarous. But then Moses conceived his law as being what he called the law of God, and not simply an instrument for the gratification of his own cruelty and terror. It is unspeakably reassuring to learn from the British official reports laid before parliament that 'due dignity was observed in carrying out the executions', and 'all possible humanity was shewn in carrying them out', and that 'the arrangements were admirable, and reflect great credit on all concerned'. As this last testimonial apparently does not refer to the victims, they are evidently officially considered not to have been concerned in the proceedings at all. Finally, Lord Cromer certifies that the Englishman in charge of the proceedings is 'a singularly humane man, and is very popular amongst the natives of Egypt by reason of the great sympathy he has always shewn for them'. It will be seen that Pariamentary Papers, Nos. 3 and 4, Egypt, 1906, are not lacking in unconscious humor. The official walrus pledges himself in every case for the kindliness of the official carpenter.

One man was actually let off, to the great danger of the British Empire perhaps. Still, as he was an epileptic, and had already had several fits in the court of Judge Lynch, the doctor said Better not; and he escaped. This was very inconvenient; for the number of floggees had been made up solely to fill the time occupied by the hangings at the rate of two floggings per hanging; and the breakdown of the arrangement through Said Suleiman Kheirallah's inconsiderate indisposition made the execution of Darweesh tedious, as he was hanging for fully quarter of an hour without any flogging to amuse his fellow villagers and the officers and men of the Inniskilling Dragoons, the military mounted police, and the mounted infantry. A few spare sentences of flogging should have been kept in hand to provide against accidents.

In any case there was not time to flog everybody, not to flog three of the floggees enough; so these three had a year's hard labor apiece in addition to their floggings. Six others were not flogged at all, but were sent to penal servitude for seven years each. One man got fifteen years. Total for the morning's work: four hanged, two to penal servitude for life, one to fifteen years penal servitude, six to seven years penal servitude, three to imprisonment for a year with hard labor and fifty lashes, and five to fifty lashes.

Lord Cromer certifies that these proceedings were 'just and necessary'. He also gives his reasons. It appears that the boasted justice introduced into Egypt by the English in 1882 was imaginary, and that the real work of coping with Egyptian disorder was done by Brigandage Commissions, composed of Egyptians. These Commissions, when an offence was reported, descended on the inculpated village; seized everybody concerned; and plied them with tortures, mentionable and unmentionable, until they accused everybody they were expected to accuse. The accused were in turn tortured until they confessed anything and everything they were accused of. They were then killed, flogged, or sent to penal servitude.

This was the reality behind the illusion that soothed us after bombarding Alexandria. The bloodless, white-gloved native courts set up to flatter our sense of imperial justice had, apparently, about as much to do with the actual government of the fellaheen as the annual court which awards the Dunmow flitch of bacon has to do with our divorce court. Eventually a Belgian judge, who was appointed Procureur-Général, exposed the true state of affairs.

Then the situation had to be faced. Order had to be maintained somehow; but the regular native courts which saved the face of the British Occupation were useless for the purpose; and the Brigandage Commissions were so abominable and demoralizing that they made more mischief than they prevented. Besides, there was Mr Wilfrid Scawen Blunt on the warpath against tyranny and torture, threatening to get questions asked in parliament. A new sort of tribunal in the nature of a court-martial had therefore to be invented to replace the Brigandage Commissions; but simple British military courts-martial, though probably the best available form of official Lynch Law, were made impossible by the jealousy of the 'loyal' (to England) Egyptians, who, it seems, rule the Occupation and bully England exactly as the 'loyal' Irish rule the Garrison and bully the Unionists nearer home. That kind of loyalty, not being a natural product, has to be purchased; and the price is an official job of some sort with a position and a salary attached. Hence we got, in 1895, a tribunal constituted in which three English officials sat with two Egyptian officials, exercising practically unlimited powers of punishment without a jury and without appeal. They represent the best of our judicial and military officialism. And what that best is may be judged by the sentences on the Denshawai villagers.

Lord Cromer's justification of the tribunal is practically that, bad as it is, the Brigandage Commissions were worse. Also (lest we should propose to carry our moral superiority any further) that the Egyptians are so accustomed to associate law and order with floggings, executions, torture and Lynch Law, that they will not respect any tribunal which does not continue these practices. This is a far-reaching argument: for instance, it suggests that Church of England missionaries might do well to adopt the rite of human sacrifice when evangelizing tribes in whose imagination that practice is inseparably bound up with religion. It suggests that the sole reason why the Denshawai tribunal did not resort to torture for the purpose of extorting confessions and evidence was that parliament might not stand it – though really a parliament which stood the executions would, one would think, stand anything. The tribunal had certainly no intention of allowing witnesses to testify against British officers; for, as it happened, the Ombashi who accompanied them on the two shooting expeditions, one Ahmed Hassan Zakzouk, aged 26, was rash enough to insist that after the shot that struck the woman, the officers fired on the mob twice. This appears in the parliamentary paper; but the French newspaper *L'Égypte* is quoted by Mr Wilfrid Scawen Blunt as reporting that Zakzouk, on being asked by one of the English judges whether he was not afraid to say such a thing, replied 'Nobody in the world is able to frighten me: the truth is the truth,' and was promptly told to stand down. Mr Blunt adds that Zakzouk was then tried for his conduct in connection with the affair before a Court of Discipline, which awarded him two years imprisonment and fifty lashes. Without rudely calling this a use of torture to intimidate anti-British witnesses, I may count on the assent of most reasonable people when I say that Zakzouk probably regards himself as having received a rather strong hint to make his evidence agreeable to the Occupation in future.

Not only was there of course no jury at the trial, but considerably less than no defence. Barristers of sufficient standing to make it very un-desirable for them to offend the Occupation were instructed to 'defend' the prisoners. Far from defending them, they paid high compliments to the Occupation as one of the choicest benefits rained by Heaven on their country, and appealed for mercy for their miserable clients, whose conduct had 'caused the unanimous indignation of all Egyptians'. 'Clemency,' they said, 'was above equity.' The Tribunal in delivering judgment remarked that 'the counsel for the defence had a full hearing: nevertheless the defence broke down completely, and all that their counsel could say on behalf of the prisoners practically amounted to an appeal to the mercy of the Court'.

Now the proper defence, if put forward, would probably have con-vinced Lord Cromer that nothing but the burning of the village and the crucifixion of all its inhabitants could preserve the British Empire. That defence was obvious enough: the village was invaded by five armed foreigners who attempted for the second time to slaughter the villagers' farming stock and carry it off; in resisting an attempt to disarm them four villagers had been wounded; the villagers had lost their tempers and knocked the invaders about; and the older men and watchmen had finally rescued the aggressors and sent them back with no worse handling than they would have got anywhere for the like misconduct.

One can imagine what would have happened to the man, prisoner or advocate, who should have dared to tell the truth in this fashion. The prisoners knew better than to attempt it. On the scaffold, Darweesh turned to his house as he stood on the trap, and exclaimed 'May God compensate us well for this world of meanness, for this world of injustice, for this world of cruelty.' If he had dared in court thus to compare God with the tribunal to the disadvantage of the latter, he would no doubt have had fifty lashes before his hanging, to teach him the greatness of the Empire. As it was, he kept his views to himself until it was too late to do anything worse to him than hang him. In court, he did as all the rest did. They lied; they denied; they set up desperate alibis; they protested they had been in the next village, or tending cattle a mile off, or threshing, or what not. One of them, when identified, said 'All men are alike.' He had only one eye. Darweesh, who had secured one of the officers' guns, declared that his enemies had come in the night and buried it in his house, where his mother sat on it, like Rachel on Laban's stolen teraphim, until she was dragged off. A pitiable business, yet not so pitiable as the virtuous indignation with which Judge Lynch, himself provable by his own judgment to be a prevaricator, hypocrite, tyrant, and coward of the first water, preened himself at its expense. When Lord Cromer, in his official apology for Judge Lynch, says that 'the prisoners had a perfectly fair trial' – not, observe, a trial as little unfair as human frailty could make it, which is the most that can be said for any trial on earth, but 'a *perfectly* fair trial' – he no doubt believes what he says; but his opinion is interesting mainly as an example of the state of his mind, and of the extent to which, after thirty years of official life in Egypt, one loses the plain sense of English words.

Lord Cromer recalls how, in the eighties, a man threatened with the courbash by a Moudir in the presence of Sir Claude MacDonald, said 'You dare not flog me now that the British are here.' 'So bold an answer,' says Lord Cromer, 'was probably due to the presence of a British officer.' What would that man say now? What does Lord Cromer say now? He deprecates 'premature endeavors to thrust Western ideas on an Eastern people', by which he means that when you are in Egypt you must do as the Egyptians do: terrorize by the lash and the scaffold. Thus does the East conquer its conquerors. In 1883 Lord Dufferin was abolishing the bastinado as 'a horrible and infamous punishment'. In 1906 Lord Cromer guarantees ferocious sentences of flogging as 'just and necessary', and can see 'nothing reprehensible in the manner in which they were carried out'. 'I have,' he adds, 'passed nearly thirty years of my life in an earnest endeavor to raise the moral and material condition of the people of Egypt. I have been assisted by a number of very capable officials, all of whom, I may say, have been animated by the same spirit as myself.' Egypt may well shudder as she reads those words. If the first thirty years have been crowned by the Denshawai incident, what will Egypt be like at the end of another thirty years of moral elevation 'animated by the same spirit'?

It is pleasanter to return to Lord Cromer's first letter on Denshawai, written to Sir Edward Grey the day after the shooting party. It says that 'orders will shortly be issued by the General prohibiting officers in the army from shooting pigeons in the future under any circumstances whatever'. But pray why this prohibition, if, as the tribunal declared, the officers were 'guests [actually *guests!*] who had done nothing to deserve blame'?

Mr Findlay is another interesting official correspondent of Sir Edward. Even after the trial, at which it had been impossible to push the medical evidence further than to say that the officer who died of sunstroke had been predisposed to it by the knocking about he had suffered and by his flight under the Egyptian sun, whilst the officers who had remained defenceless in the hands of the villagers were in court, alive and well, Mr Findlay writes that the four hanged men were 'convicted of a brutal and premeditated murder', and complains that 'the native press disregards the fact' and 'is being conducted with such an absolute disregard for the truth as to make it evident that large sums of money have been expended'. Mr Findlay is also a bit of a philosopher. 'The Egyptian, being a fatalist,' he says, 'does not greatly fear death, and there is therefore much to be said for flogging as a judicial punishment in Egypt.' Logically, then, the four hanged men ought to have been flogged instead. But Mr Findlay does not draw that conclusion. Logic is not his strong point: he is a man of feeling, and a very nervous one at that. 'I do not believe that this brutal attack on British officers had anything directly to do with political animosity. It is, however, due to the insubordinate spirit which has been sedulously fostered during the last year by unscrupulous and interested agitators.' Again, 'it is my duty to warn you of the deplorable effect which is being produced in Egypt by the fact that Members of Parliament have seriously called in question the unanimous sentence passed by a legally constituted Court, of which the best English and the best native Judge were members. This fact will, moreover, supply the lever which has, up to the present, been lacking to the venal agitators who are at the head of the so-called patriotic party.' I find Mr Findlay irresistible, so exquisitely does he give us the measure and flavor of officialism. 'A few days after the Denshawai affray some native stoned and severely injured an irrigation inspector. Two days ago three natives knocked a soldier off his donkey and kicked him in the stomach: his injuries are serious. In the latter case theft appears to have been the motive. My object in mentioning these instances is to shew the results to be expected if once respect for the law is shaken. Should the present state of things continue, and, still more, should the agitation in this country find support at home, the date is not far distant when the necessity will arise for bringing in a press law and for considerably increasing the army of occupation.' Just think of it! In a population of nearly ten million, one irrigation inspector is stoned. The Denshawai executions are then carried out to make the law respected. The result is that three natives knock a soldier off his donkey and rob him. Thereupon Mr Findlay, appalled at the bankruptcy of civilization, sees nothing for it now but suppression of the native newspapers and a considerable increase in the army of occupation! And Lord Cromer writes 'All I need say is that I concur generally in Mr Findlay's remarks, and that, had I remained in Egypt, I should in every respect have adopted the same course as that which he pursued.'

But I must resolutely shut this rich parliamentary paper. I have extracted enough to paint the picture, and enforce my warning to England that if her Empire means ruling the world as Denshawai has been ruled in 1906 – and that, I am afraid, is what the Empire does mean to the main body of our aristocratic-military caste and to our Jingo plutocrats – then there can be no more sacred and urgent political duty on earth than the disruption, defeat, and suppression of the Empire, and, incidentally, the humanization of its supporters by the sternest lessons of that adversity which comes finally to institutions which make themselves abhorred by the aspiring will of humanity towards divinity. As for the Egyptians, any man cradled by the Nile who, after the Denshawai incident, will ever voluntarily submit to British rule, or accept any bond with us except the bond of a Federation of free and equal states, will deserve the worst that Lord Cromer can consider 'just and necessary' for him. That is what you get by attempting to prove your supremacy by the excesses of frightened soldiers and denaturalized officials instead of by courageous helpfulness and moral superiority.

In any case let no Englishman who is content to leave Abd-el-Nebi and his twenty-year-old neighbor in penal servitude for life, and to plume himself on the power to do it, pretend to be fit to govern either my country or his own. The responsibility cannot be confined to the tribunal and to the demoralized officials of the Occupation. The House of Commons had twentyfour hours clear notice, with the telegraph under the hand of Sir Edward Grey, to enable it to declare that England was a civilized Power and would not stand these barbarous lashings and vindictive hangings. Yet Mr Dillon, representing the Irish party, which well knows what British Occupation and Findlay 'loyalism' mean, protested in vain. Sir Edward, on behalf of the new Liberal Government (still simmering with virtuous indignation at the flogging of Chinamen and the military executions in South Africa in the forced presence of the victims' families under the late Imperialist Government), not only permitted and defended the Denshawai executions, but appealed to the House almost passionately not to criticize or repudiate them, on the ground – how incredible it now appears! – that Abd-el-Nebi and Hassan Mahfouz and Darweesh and the rest were the fuglemen of a gigantic Moslem plot to rise against Christendom in the name of the Prophet and sweep Christendom out of Africa and Asia by a colossal second edition of the Indian Mutiny. That this idiotic romance, gross and ridiculous as the lies of Falstaff, should have imposed on any intelligent and politically experienced human being, is strange enough – though the secret shame of revolted humanity will make cabinet ministers snatch at fantastic excuses – but what humanity will not forgive our foreign secretary for is his failure to see that even if such a conspiracy really existed, England should have faced it and fought it bravely by honorable means, instead of wildly lashing and strangling a handful of poor peasants to scare Islam into terrified submission. Were I abject enough to grant to Sir Edward Grey as valid that main asset of 'thinking Imperially', the conviction that we are all going to be murdered, I should still suggest to him that we can at least die like gentlemen? Might I even be so personal as to say that the reason for giving him a social position and political opportunities that are denied to his tradesmen is that he is supposed to understand better than they that honor is worth its danger and its cost, and that life is worthless without honor? It is true that Sir John Falstaff did not think so; but Sir John is hardly a model for Sir Edward. Yet even Sir John would have had enough gumption to see that the Denshawai panic was more dangerous to the Empire than the loss of ten pitched battles.

As cowardice is highly infectious, would it not be desirable to supersede officials who, after years of oriental service, have lost the familiar art of concealing their terrors? I am myself a sedentary literary civilian, constitutionally timid; but I find it possible to keep up appearances, and can even face the risk of being run over, or garotted, or burnt out in London without shrieking for martial law, suppression of the newspapers, exemplary flogging and hanging of motor-bus drivers, and compulsory police service. Why are soldiers and officials on foreign service so much more cowardly than citizens? Is it not clearly because the whole Imperial military system of coercion and terrorism is unnatural, and that the truth formulated by William Morris that 'no man is good enough to be another man's master' is true also of nations, and very specially true of those plutocrat-ridden Powers which have of late stumbled into an enormous increase of material wealth without having made any intelligent provision for its proper distribution and administration?

However, the economic reform of the Empire is a long business, whereas the release of Abd-el-Nebi and his neighbors is a matter of the stroke of a pen, once public opinion is shamed into activity. I fear I have stated their case very unfairly and inadequately, because I am hampered, as an Irishman, by my implacable hostility to English domination. Mistrusting my own prejudices, I have taken the story from the two parliamentary papers in which our officials have done their utmost to whitewash the tribunals and the pigeon-shooting party, and to blackwash the villagers. Those who wish to have it told to them by an Englishman of unquestionable personal and social credentials, and an intimate knowledge of Egypt and the Egyptians, can find it in Mr Wilfrid Scawen Blunt's pamphlet entitled 'Atrocities of British Rule in Egypt'. When they have read it they will appreciate my forbearance; and when I add that English rule in Ireland has been 'animated by the same spirit' (I thank Lord Cromer for the phrase) as English rule in Egypt, and that this is the inevitable spirit of all coercive military rule, they will perhaps begin to understand why Home Rule is a necessity not only for Ireland, but for all constituents of those Federations of Commonwealths which are now the only permanently practicable form of Empire.

POSTSCRIPT. These sheets had passed through the press when the news came of Lord Cromer's resignation. As he accuses himself of failing health, he will perhaps forgive me for accusing him of failing judgment, and for suggesting that his retirement from office might well be celebrated in Egypt by the retirement, at his intercession, of Abd-el-Nabi and the rest from penal servitude.

A YEAR LATER

It may be a relief to some of my readers to learn that very shortly after the publication of the above account of the Denshawai atrocity, I received a private assurance that Abd-el-Nebi and his fellow-prisoners would be released on the following New Year's Day, which is the customary occasion in Egypt for such acts of grace and clemency as the Occupation may allow the Khedive to perform, and that in the meantime their detention would not be rigorous. As the hanged men could not be un-hanged nor the flogged men unflogged, this was all that could be done. I am bound to add, in justice to the Government, that this was, as far as I could ascertain, an act of pure conscience on the part of the Cabinet; for there was no sign of any serious pressure of public opinion. One or two newspapers seemed to be amused at my calling the Denshawai villagers Denshavians; but they shewed no other interest in the matter: another illustration of how hopeless it is to induce one modern nation, pre-occupied as it necessarily is with its own affairs, to take any real interest in the welfare of another, even when it professes to govern that other in a superior manner for its good. Sir Edward Grey's reputation as a great Minister for Foreign Affairs was not shaken in the least: the eulogies which were heaped on him by both parties increased in volume; and an attempt which I made to call attention to the real character of the Anglo-Russian agreement as to Persia, which was held up as a masterpiece of his diplomacy (I was apparently the only person who had taken the trouble to read it) had no effect. Not until Sir Edward ventured to threaten a really formidable European Power in 1911, and threatened it successfully from his point of view, did a sudden and violent agitation against him spring up. Until then, men of both parties idolized him without knowing why, just as they had formerly idolized Lord Cromer and Lord Milner without knowing why. They will now very possibly turn on him and rend him, also without knowing why. The one thing they will not do is to blame themselves, which is the only blaming that can be of any profit to them.

Preface to the
Home Rule Edition of
1912

[When Shaw reprinted this Preface in the Collected Edition of his works in 1930, he placed it before the original Preface and added an explanatory note. The text has now been placed in its proper chronological order. The prefatory note has been retained without editorial revision.]

(I reprint this interim preface after much hesitation. It is based on two confident political assumptions that have since been not merely disproved but catastrophically shattered.

The first was that Parliament in 1912 was still what it had been in the heyday of Gladstonian Liberalism, when it was utterly inconceivable that an Act of constitutional reform which had been duly passed and assented-to by the Crown could be dropped into the waste paper basket because a handful of ladies and gentlemen objected to it, and the army officers' messes blustered mutinously against it.

The second assumption was that Ireland was politically one and indivisible, and, consequently, that when Home Rule came, as it was evident it must come, the Protestants of Ireland must stand together and make the best of it. The possibility of a Partition by which Belfast Protestantism should accept Home Rule for itself in a concentration camp and thus abandon its co-religionists outside the camp to what must then inevitably become a Roman Catholic Home Rule Government of the rest of Ireland, was undreamt of.

How both these things nevertheless happened I have described in a postscript to the original preface which will be found on a later page. Readers who skip to that preface will lose nothing by missing this one except a possibly instructive example of how our eternal march into the future must always be a blindfold march. I guessed ahead, and guessed wrongly, whilst stupider and more ignorant fellow-pilgrims guessed rightly.)

John Bull's Other Island was written when a Unionist Government was in power, and had been in power with one brief interval for twenty years. The reason for this apparent eclipse of Home Rule was that the Liberal Party had during that period persisted in assuring the English people anxiously that it had no intention of doing anything for England (its object being to shew its abhorrence of Socialism) and that it cared for nothing but Home Rule in Ireland. Now as the English electors, being mostly worse off than the Irish, were anxious to have something done to alleviate their own wretched condition, they steadily voted for the Unionist Party (not because it was Unionist, but because it cared more for England than for Ireland), except on one occasion in 1893, when the Liberals put all their Home Rule tracts in the fire, and fought on a program of English Social Reform, known as the Newcastle Program, drawn up by my friend and Fabian colleague, Mr Sidney Webb, and ingeniously foisted on the Liberals by myself and other Fabians disguised as artless Gladstonian members of certain little local caucuses which called themselves Liberal and Radical Associations, and were open to any passer-by who might astonish them by seeming to take an interest in their routine of bleeding candidates for registration expenses and local subscriptions. The program won the election for the Home Rulers. It was a close thing; but it won it. The Liberals then dropped it; and Lord Rosebery made his famous discovery that programs are a mistake, a view which, though supported with deep conviction by his Party, which still had no desire to do or mean or understand anything that could conceivably benefit anyone in England, had the immediate effect of extinguishing its noble author politically, and sending his party back into opposition for another ten years, at the end of which the Unionists, quite as ignorant of what the people of England were thinking about as Lord Rosebery, entered upon an impassioned defence of the employment of Chinese labor in South Africa without considering the fact that every one of their arguments was equally valid for the introduction of Chinese labor into Lancashire. And as the people of Lancashire were concerned about Lancashire and not at all about South Africa, the Unionist Party followed Lord Rosebery into the shades.

One consequence of this political swing of the pendulum was that John Bull's Other Island, which had up to that moment been a topical play, immediately became a historical one. Broadbent is no longer up-to-date. His *bête noir*, Mr Joseph Chamberlain, has retired from public life. The controversies about Tariff Reform, the Education and Licensing Bills, and the South African war, have given way to the far more vital questions raised by Mr Lloyd George's first unskilful essays in Collectivism, and to the agitation for Votes for Women. Broadbent is still strong on the question of Persia: stronger than he was on that of Armenia (probably because Persia is further off); but there is little left of the subjects that excited him in 1904 except Home Rule. And Home Rule is to be disposed of this year.

The Government will no doubt be glad to get rid of it. The English people, with prices up and wages down, care less, if possible, than they ever did about it. Even the governing classes are feeling the pressure of the Home Rule agitations in Egypt and India more than in Ireland; for the Irish, now confident that their battle is won, are keeping comparatively quiet, whilst in the East the question is in the acute stage in which the Government has to explain that really very few people have had confessions extorted by torture in the police stations, and that if the natives would only be reasonable and recognize the advantages of British rule, and their own utter unfitness for self-government, there would be no need to imprison nationalists either in India or Egypt; so that, in effect, the natives have themselves to thank for whatever unpleasantness may happen to them.

The only considerable body of Englishmen really concerned about Home Rule except as a Party question, are those members of the Free Churches, vulgarly called Dissenters or Nonconformists, who believe that the effect of Home Rule would be to deliver Ireland into the hands of the Roman Catholic Church, which they regard as The Scarlet Woman. It is clearly not a very deeply considered apprehension, because there is not a country in the world, not even Spain, where the people are so completely in the hands of the Roman Catholic Church as they are in Ireland under English rule and because of English rule. In the non-Protestant Christian countries which are politically independent, the clericals are struggling, not to regain their lost supremacy (that survives only in Ireland), but for their houses, their property, their right to live in the country they were born in, and to have the political weight due to their merits; for they have merits: the priest is not so black as he is painted in all free countries nowadays. But our Free Churchmen are too much afraid of the Pope, and of the confessional, and of the priest in the house, to see how weak these forces are in the face of democracy. Also, they are not all well off enough to buy plays in six-shilling, or even in eighteenpenny volumes. Therefore, I think it opportune to issue this cheap edition of John Bull's Other Island this Home Rule Year, because its preface was written by an Irishman of Protestant family and Protestant prejudices, and shews that the one way in which the power of the priest can be kept within its proper limits in Ireland is by setting the Irish people free to take it in hand themselves without seeming to be treacherously taking the side of England against their own country.

Still more needed is this cheap edition in Ireland, where nobody can well afford to pay more than sixpence for anything, since, if I may put it elliptically, the only people in Ireland who can afford more than sixpence are those who live in England. I should like to call the attention of my nervous fellow Protestants in Ireland to the fact that in Italy, the centre of Roman Catholicism, the Pope is in a position closely resembling what that of Louis XVI would have been during the first years of the French Revolution if he, like the Pope, had had no wife to bring him to the scaffold by tempting him to betray his country to a foreign foe. Also that in France, in spite of the revocation of the Edict of Nantes by the Roman Catholic Church at the height of its power, the Huguenots have always wielded, and still wield today, a power that is out of all proportion to their comparative numbers, and even, I am afraid I must add, to their merits. The Huguenot of Ulster is a coward only when he breaks his own backbone by taking the part of a foreign country against his own. Shut him up in Derry with an English King besieging him, and he does not shriek for the Germans to come and help him as if the thumbscrews of the Spanish Armada were already on his hands; he chalks up No Surrender merrily, and puts up one of the famous fights of history. After all, what is the use of protesting that you will not be governed from Rome if the alternative is to be governed from London? The great Protestant Irishmen have been all the more powerful because they loved Ireland better, not only than Rome, but than England. Why was it that the priests had no power to impose a Roman Catholic Leader on the Home Rule movement instead of Parnell? Simply because Parnell was so proud of his Irish birthright that he would rather have been one of even a persecuted minority in an Irish parliament than the Premier of an English Cabinet. He was not afraid of his countrymen: he knew that Protestantism could hold its own only too well in a free Ireland; and even if he had not known it he would have taken his chance rather than sell his birthright and his country. It is the essential dishonor of acting as a foreign garrison in a land where they are not foreigners that makes the position of the Orangemen so impossible, and breaks in them the spirit that animates every man in Europe who is fighting for a minority; and what man of any dignity today is not one of a minority that cries in the wilderness against one or other of the manifold iniquities and falsehoods of our civilization? I think if I as a Home Ruler (and many other less orthodox things) can live in England and hold my own in a minority which on some very sensitive points reaches the odds of about 1 to 48,000,000, an Ulster Orangeman should be able to face Home Rule without his knees knocking shamefully in the face of a contemptuous England which despises him none the less because his cowardice seems to serve her own turn.

There are, I know, men and women who are political perverts by nature. The supreme misfortune of being born with one's natural instincts turned against nature by a freak of nature is a phenomenon that occurs politically as well as physiologically. There are Poles who are devoted with all their soul to Russia and the maintenance of Russian rule in Poland, Persians who are risking their lives to introduce it in Persia, Indians and Egyptians who are ready to sacrifice all they possess for England and English rule. And it is not to be denied that among these are persons of high character and remarkable ability, comparing very favorably with the dregs of the nationalist movements, which, just because they are national and normal, are made up of all sorts, and consequently have dregs: pretty nasty ones too. For that matter, if ever a Book of Spies be written, it will include examples of courage, conviction, perseverance, and ability, that will almost persuade shallow people that spies are the real heroes of military history. Even in more personal relations, natural passion cannot pretend to inspire more intense devotion than perverted passion. But when all is said, the pervert, however magnificently he may conduct his campaign against nature, remains abhorrent. When Napoleon, though he boasted of having made peers and marshals of peasants and ostlers, drew the line at promoting a spy, he followed a universal instinct and a sound one. When the Irish Catholic who, feeling bitterly that the domination of the priest is making his own lot hopeless, nevertheless stands shoulder to shoulder with the priest for Home Rule against Dublin Castle, he is behaving naturally and rightly. When the Orangeman sacrifices his nationality to his hatred of the priest, and fights against his own country for its conqueror, he is doing something for which, no matter how bravely he fights, history and humanity will never forgive him: English history and humanity, to their credit be it said, least of all.

Please do not suppose for a moment that I propose that the Irish Protestant should submit to the Irish Roman Catholic. I reproach the Irish Roman Catholic for his submission to Rome exactly as I reproach the Orangeman for his submission to England. If Catholicism is to be limited in Ireland by any geographical expression (in which case it ceases to be Catholic) let it be Irish Catholicism, not Italian Catholicism. Let us maintain our partnership with Rome as carefully as our partnership with England; but let it be, in the one case as in the other, a free partnership. But the Irish Catholics are not Italian in their politics. They do not oppose Home Rule; and that gives them the right to the support of every Irish Protestant until Home Rule is achieved. After that, let us by all means begin a civil war next day if we are fools enough. A war for an idea may be a folly; but it is not a dishonor. Both parties would be fighting for Ireland; and though the slaying of an Irishman by an Irishman for Ireland may be a tragedy – may be even a crime to those who think that all war is crime – at least it is not unnatural crime, like the slaying of an Irishman by an Irishman for England's sake. There will, of course, be no war of religion: I have shewn in this book that the Protestant under Home Rule will be far safer and stronger than he is today; but even if there were, that is the way to look at it.

The question is still more important for England than for Ireland, in spite of England's indifference to it. In Ireland we are still sane: we do not sneer at our country as 'Little Ireland', and cheer for a doubtful commercial speculation called The Empire which we could not point out accurately on the map, and which is populated by such an overwhelming majority of what an Irish peasant would call 'black heathens', that they force us to punish our own missionaries for asking them to buy and read The Bible, and compel the Protestant Passive Resisters, who will be sold up rather than pay a rate to maintain a Church school, to pay without a murmur for the establishment of the Roman Catholic Church in Malta. Formerly 'Little England', the 'right little, tight little Island', despised Spain for her imperial policy, and saw her lose her place, not only among the empires, but even among the nations, with self-satisfied superiority. Today England is letting herself be dragged into the path of Spain. She dreams of nothing but the old beginning: an Invincible Armada. Spain reckoned without the Lord of Hosts, who scattered that Invincible Armada for Little England. The modern Imperialist does not believe in the Lord of Hosts; but the Armada was defeated for all that, though England's fleet was far more inferior to it than the German fleet will ever again be to the English fleet. The Lord of Hosts may not be quite the sort of power that Philip of Spain conceived it to be: many of us are dropping the personal pronoun, as I have just dropped it lest I should be prosecuted for superstition by the Society for the Encouragement of Cruelty to Animals; but it can still send bigger fleets to the bottom than England can build, and exalt smaller nations than England ever was above drifting congeries of derelict regions held desperately together by terrified soldiers trying to wave half a dozen flags all at once in the name of Empire: a name that every man who has ever felt the sacredness of his own native soil to him, and thus learnt to regard that feeling in other men as something holy and inviolable, spits out of his mouth with enormous contempt.

Not that I have any delusions about Drake and his Elizabethan comrades: they were pirates and slave-traders, not a whit better than the Algerine corsair who shared with them what modern idiots call 'the command of the sea' (much the sea cares about their command!); but it is better to be a pirate trading in slaves out of sheer natural wickedness than a bankrupt in a cocked hat, doing the same things, and worse, against your own conscience, because you are paid for it and are afraid to do anything else. Drake thought nothing of burning a Spanish city; but he was not such a fool as to suppose that if he told off some of his crew to stay and govern that Spanish city by force when it was rebuilt, all the reasonable inhabitants of that town would recognize the arrangement as an enormous improvement, and be very much obliged to him, which is the modern Imperial idea. To singe the King of Spain's beard; pick his pocket; and run away, was, in the absence of any international police, a profitable bit of sport, if a rascally one; but if Drake had put a chain round the King's neck and led him round a prisoner for the rest of his life, he would have suffered as much by such a folly as the King, and probably died sooner of worry, anxiety, expense, and loss through the neglect of his own proper affairs, than the King would have died of captivity. Bermondsey goes to the dogs whilst those whose business it is to govern it are sitting on Bengal;

and the more Bengal kicks, the more Bermondsey is neglected, except by the tax collector. The notion that the way to prosper is to insist on managing everybody else's affairs is, on the face of it, a fool's notion. It is at bottom the folly of the ignorant simpletons who long to be kings and chiefs because they imagine that a king or chief is an idle voluptuary with lots of money, leisure, and power over others, to use irresponsibly for his own amusement.

In short, then, the future is not to the empires, but to federations of self-governing nations, exactly as, within these nations, the future is not to Capitalist Oligarchies, but to Collectivist organizations of free and equal citizens. In short, to Commonwealths.

In expressing this irresistible sentiment of nationality with all the rhetoric to which it lends itself, I am not forgetting that there are international rights as well as national ones. We are not only natives within our own frontiers but inheritors of the earth. England has rights in Ireland as Ireland has rights in England. I demand of every nation right of ingress and egress, roads, police, an efficient post office, and, in reason, freedom of conscience. I am prepared to steam-roller Tibet if Tibet persist in refusing me my international rights. If the Moors and Arabs cannot or will not secure these common human conditions for me in North Africa, I am quite prepared to co-operate with the French, the Italians, and the Spaniards in Morocco, Algeria, Tunisia, and Tripoli, with the Russians in Siberia, with all three and the English and Germans as well in Africa, or with the Americans in the hunting grounds of the red man, to civilize these places; though I know as well as anyone that there are many detestable features in our civilization, many virtues in village and tribal communities, and a very large alloy indeed of brigandage in our explorations and colonizations.

I know also that what compels us to push our frontiers farther and farther into regions we call barbarous is the necessity of policing, not the barbarians, but the European dregs and riffraff who set up little hells of anarchy and infamy just beyond the border, and thus compel us to advance and rope them in, step by step, no matter how much we are adding to that 'white man's burden', which is none the less a real thing because it is not specially a white man's burden any more than it is specially an Englishman's burden, as most of Mr Kipling's readers seem to interpret it. Tribes must make themselves into nations before they can claim the rights of nations; and this they can do only by civilization.

Also I cannot deny that the exclusion of the Chinese from America and Australia is a violation of international right which the Chinese will be perfectly justified in resisting by arms as soon as they feel strong enough. If nations are to limit immigration, inter-marriage with foreigners, and even international trade by tariffs, it had better be done by international law than by arbitrary national force as at present. It will be seen that I am under no delusion as to the freedom of Nationalism from abuse. I know that there are abuses in England which would not exist if she were governed by Germany, and that there will no doubt be abuses in Ireland under Home Rule which do not exist under English rule, just as things have been done under the Irish Local Government Act that the old oligarchical grand juries would not have tolerated. There are, indeed, a hundred horses on which I could ride off if I wished to shirk the main issue. But when all is said, it is so certain that in the long run all civilized nations must at the same time become more dependent one on another and do their own governing work themselves, that if Ireland refused Home Rule now, it would sooner or later be forced on her by England because England will need all her time and political energy for her own affairs when once she realizes that the day for letting them slide and muddling through is past.

LONDON
19th January 1912

TWENTYFOUR YEARS LATER

The sequel to these events confirmed my unheeded warning with a sanguinary completeness of which I had no prevision. At Easter 1916 a handful of Irishmen seized the Dublin Post Office and proclaimed an Irish Republic, with one of their number, a schoolmaster named Pearse, as President. If all Ireland had risen at this gesture it would have been a serious matter for England, then up to her neck in the war against the Central Empires. But there was no response: the gesture was a complete failure. All that was necessary was to blockade the Post Office until its microscopic republic was starved out and made ridiculous. What actually happened would be incredible if there were not so many living witnesses of it. From a battery planted at Trinity College (the Irish equivalent of Oxford University), and from a warship in the river Liffey, a bombardment was poured on the centre of the city which reduced more than a square mile of it to such a condition that when, in the following year, I was taken through Arras and Ypres to shew me what the German artillery had done to these cities in two and a half years, I laughed and said, 'You should see what the British artillery did to my native city in a week.' It would not be true to say that not one stone was left upon another; for the marksmanship was so bad that the Post Office itself was left standing amid a waste of rubbish heaps; and enough scraps of wall were left for the British Army, which needed recruits, to cover with appeals to the Irish to remember Belgium lest the fate of Louvain should befall their own hearths and homes.

Having thus worked up a harebrained romantic adventure into a heroic episode in the struggle for Irish freedom, the victorious artillerists proceeded to kill their prisoners of war in a drawn-out string of executions. Those who were executed accordingly became not only national heroes, but the martyrs whose blood was the seed of the present Irish Free State. Among those who escaped was its first President. Nothing more blindly savage, stupid, and terror-mad could have been devised by England's worst enemies. It was a very characteristic example of the mentality produced by the conventional gentleman-militarist education at Marlborough and Sandhurst and the conventional gentleman-diplomatist education at Eton and Oxford, Harrow and Cambridge. Is it surprising that the Russian Soviet Government, though fanatically credulous as to the need for popular education, absolutely refused to employ as teachers anyone who had been touched by the equivalent public school and university routine in Russia, and stuck to its resolution even at the cost of carrying on for some years with teachers who were hardly a day ahead of their pupils?

But the Post Office episode was eclipsed by an event which was much more than an episode, as it shattered the whole case for parliamentary government throughout the world. The Irish Nationalists, after thirty years of constitutional procedure in the British Parliament, had carried an Act to establish Irish Home Rule, as it was then called, which duly received the royal assent and became a statute of the realm. Immediately the British officers on service in Ireland mutinied, refusing to enforce the

Act or operate against the northern Orangemen who were openly arming themselves to resist it. They were assured of support by their fellow-officers at home. The Act was suspended after prominent English statesmen had taken part in the military manoeuvres of the Orangemen. The Prime Minister publicly pledged himself that Belfast, the Orange capital, would not in any case be coerced. In short, the Act was shelved under a threat of civil war; and the Clan na Gael, which in America had steadfastly maintained that the constitutional movement was useless, as England would in the last resort repudiate the constitution and hold Ireland against the Irish by physical force, and had been rebuked, lectured, and repudiated by the parliamentary Home Rulers for a whole generation for saying so, was justified. The Catholic Irish accordingly armed themselves and drilled as Volunteers in spite of the hostility of the Government, which meanwhile gave every possible assistance to the parallel preparations of the Orangemen. An Irish parliament (or Dail) sat in Dublin and claimed to be the national government. Irish courts were set up for the administration of Irish justice; Irish order was kept by Irish police; Irish taxes were collected by Irish officials; and British courts were boycotted. Upon this interesting but hopeless attempt to ignore British rule the Government let loose a specially recruited force (known to history as the Black and Tans) with *carte blanche* to kill, burn, and destroy, save only that they must stop short of rapine. They wrecked the Irish courts and produced a state of anarchy. They struck at the Irish through the popular co-operative stores and creameries, which they burnt. The people found a civil leader in Arthur Griffiths and a military one in Michael Collins. The Black and Tans had the British Government at their back: Collins had the people at his back. He threatened that for every creamery or co-operative store or cabin or cottage burnt by the Black and Tans he would burn two country houses of the Protestant gentry. The country houses that were not burnt were raided at night and laid under contribution for needed supplies. If the occupants reported the raid, the house was burnt. The Black and Tans and the ordinary constabulary were treated as enemies in uniform: that is, they were shot at sight and their stations burnt; or they were ambushed and killed in petty battles. Those who gave warnings or information of any helpful kind to them were mercilessly executed without privilege of sex or benefit of clergy. Collins, with allies in every street and hamlet, proved able to carry out his threat.

He won the crown of the Reign of Terror; and the position of the Protestant gentry became unbearable.

Thus by fire and bullet, murder and torture and devastation, a situation was produced in which the British Government had either to capitulate at the cost of a far more complete concession of self-government to Ireland than that decreed by the repudiated Home Rule Act, or to let loose the military strength of England in a Cromwellian reconquest, massacre, and replantation which it knew that public opinion in England and America would not tolerate; for some of the most conspicuous English champions of Ulster warned the Government that they could stand no more of the Black and Tan terrorism. And so we settled the Irish Question, not as civilized and reasonable men should have settled it, but as dogs settle a dispute over a bone.

Future historians will probably see in these catastrophes a ritual of human sacrifice without which the savages of the twentieth century could not effect any redistribution of political power or wealth. Nothing was learnt from Denshawai or the Black and Tan terror. In India, which is still struggling for self-government, and obviously must finally have it, a military panic led to the cannonading of a forbidden public meeting at Amritsar, the crowd being dealt with precisely as if it were a body of German shocktroops rushing the British trenches in Flanders. In London the police would have broken a score or two of heads and dragged a handful of ringleaders to the police courts. And there was the usual combination of mean spite with hyperbolical violence. Indians were forced to crawl past official buildings on their hands and knees. The effect was to make British imperial rule ridiculous in Europe, and implacably resented in India.

In Egypt the British domination died of Denshawai; but at its deathbed the British Sirdar was assassinated, whereupon the British Government, just then rather drunk after a sweeping election victory secured by an anti-Russian scare, announced to an amazed world that it was going to cut off the Nile at its source and destroy Egypt by stopping its water supply. Of course nothing happened but an ignominious climb down; but the incident illustrates my contention that our authority, when it is too far flung (as our patriotic rhapsodists put it), goes stark mad at the periphery if a pin drops. As to what further panics and atrocities will ensue before India is left to govern itself as much as Ireland and Egypt now are I am in the dark until the event enlightens me. But on the folly of allowing military counsels to prevail in political settlements I may point to the frontiers established by the victors after the war of 1914–18. Almost every one of these frontiers has a new war implicit in it, because the soldier recognizes no ethnographical, linguistic, or moral boundaries: he demands a line that he can defend, or rather that Napoleon or Wellington could have defended; for he has not yet learnt to think of offence and defence in terms of airplanes which ignore his Waterloo ridges. And the inevitable nationalist rebellions against these military frontiers, and the atrocities by which they are countered, are in full swing as I write.

Meanwhile, John Bull's Other Island, though its freedom has destroyed all the romantic interest that used to attach to it, has become at last highly interesting to the student of political science as an experiment in political structure. Protestant Ulster, which armed against the rest of Ireland and defied the British Parliament to the cry of 'We wont have it,' meaning that they would die in the last ditch singing 'O God, our help in ages past' rather than suffer or tolerate Home Rule, is now suffering and indeed hugging Home Rule on a much more homely scale than the Home Rulers ever demanded or dreamt of; for it has a Belfast Home Rule Parliament instead of an Irish one. And it has allowed Catholic Ireland to secure the Irish parliament. Thus, of the two regional parliaments which have been established on a sectarian basis, Protestant Ulster has been left with the smaller. Now it happens that Protestant Ulster is industrial Ireland and Catholic Ireland agricultural Ireland. And throughout the world for a century past the farmer, the peasant, and the Catholic have been the bulwark of the industrial capitalists against the growing political power of the industrial proletariat organized in trade unions, Labor parties, and the ubiquitous sodalities of that new ultra-Catholic Church called Socialism.

From this defensive alliance the Ulster employers, blinded by an obsolete bigotry and snobbery, have deliberately cut themselves off. In my preface of 1906, and again in my 1912 preface to a sixpenny edition of this play called the Home Rule edition, I exhorted the Protestants to take their chance, trust their grit, and play their part in a single parliament ruling an undivided Ireland. They did not take my advice. Probably they did not even read it, being too deeply absorbed in the History of Maria Monk, or the latest demonstration that all the evil in the world is the work of an underground conspiracy entitled by them 'the Jesuits'. It is a pity they did not begin their political education, as I began mine, by reading Karl Marx. It is true that I had occasion to point out that Marx was not infallible; but he left me with a very strong disposition to back the economic situation to control all the other situations, religious, nationalist, or romantic, in the long run. And so I do not despair of seeing Protestant Ulster seeking the alliance it repudiated. The Northern Parliament will not merge into the Oireachtas; for until both of them are superseded by a completely modernized central government, made for action and not for obstruction, they will remain more effective as regional parliaments than they would be as national ones; but they will soon have to take counsel together through conferences which will recur until they become a permanent institution and finally develop into what the Americans call Congress, or Federal Government of the whole island. No doubt this will be received in Belfast (if noticed at all) with shouts of 'We wont have it.' But I have heard that cry before, and regard it as a very hopeful sign that they will have it gladly enough when they have the luck to get it.

AYOT ST LAWRENCE,
   November 1929

John Bull's Other Island

Composition begun 17 June 1904; completed 23 August 1904. Published in *John Bull's Other Island, How He Lied to Her Husband, Major Barbara*, 1907. Revised text in Collected Edition, 1930. First presented at the Royal Court Theatre, London, on 1 November 1904, for six matinées.

Broadbent	*Louis Calvert*
Larry Doyle	*J. L. Shine*
Tim Haffigan	*Percival Stevens*
Hodson	*Nigel Playfair*
Peter Keegan	*Granville Barker*
Patsy Farrell	*Graham Browne*
Father Dempsey	*Charles Daly*
Corney Doyle	*F. Cremlin*
Barney Doran	*Wilfred Shine*
Matthew Haffigan	*A. E. George*
Aunt Judy	*Agnes Thomas*
Nora	*Ellen O'Malley*

Period – The Present. London and Ireland

ACT I *Office of Broadbent and Doyle, Civil Engineers, Great George Street, Westminster*

ACT II Scene 1: *Roscullen Hill*
Scene 2: *The Round Tower*

ACT III *The Grass Plot before Corney Doyle's House*

ACT IV Scene 1: *The Parlor at Corney Doyle's*
Scene 2: *Roscullen Hill*

ACT I

Great George Street, Westminster, is the address of Doyle and Broadbent, civil engineers. On the threshold one reads that the firm consists of Mr Laurence Doyle and Mr Thomas Broadbent, and that their rooms are on the first floor. Most of these rooms are private; for the partners, being bachelors and bosom friends, live there; and the door marked Private, next the clerks' office, is their domestic sitting room as well as their reception room for clients. Let me describe it briefly from the point of view of a sparrow on the window sill. The outer door is in the opposite wall, close to the right hand corner. Between this door and the left hand corner is a hatstand and a table consisting of large drawing boards on trestles, with plans, rolls of tracing paper, mathematical instruments, and other draughtsman's accessories on it. In the left hand wall is the fireplace, and the door of an inner room between the fireplace and our observant sparrow. Against the right hand wall is a filing cabinet, with a cupboard on it, and, nearer, a tall office desk and stool for one person. In the middle of the room a large double writing table is set across, with a chair at each end for the two partners. It is a room which no woman would tolerate, smelling of tobacco, and much in need of repapering, repainting, and recarpeting; but this is the effect of bachelor untidiness and indifference, not want of means; for nothing that Doyle and Broadbent themselves have purchased is cheap; nor is anything they want lacking. On the walls hang a large map of South America, a pictorial advertisement of a steamship company, an impressive portrait of Gladstone, and several caricatures of Mr Balfour as a rabbit and Mr Chamberlain as a fox by Francis Carruthers Gould.

At twenty minutes to five o'clock on a summer afternoon in 1904, the room is empty. Presently the outer door is opened, and a valet comes in laden with a large Gladstone bag and a strap of rugs. He carries them into the inner room. He is a respectable valet, old enough to have lost all alacrity and acquired an air of putting up patiently with a great deal of trouble and indifferent health. The luggage belongs to Broadbent, who enters after the valet. He pulls off his overcoat and hangs it with his hat on the stand. Then he comes to the writing table and looks through the letters waiting there for him. He is a robust, full-blooded, energetic man in the prime of life, sometimes eager and credulous, sometimes shrewd and roguish, sometimes portentously solemn, sometimes jolly *and impetuous, always buoyant and irresistible, mostly likeable, and enormously absurd in his most earnest moments. He bursts open his letters with his thumb, and glances through them, flinging the envelopes about the floor with reckless untidiness whilst he talks to the valet.*

BROADBENT [*calling*] Hodson.

HODSON [*in the bedroom*] Yes sir.

BROADBENT. Dont unpack. Just take out the things Ive worn; and put in clean things.

HODSON [*appearing at the bedroom door*] Yes sir. [*He turns to go back into the bedroom*].

BROADBENT. And look here! [*Hodson turns again*]. Do you remember where I put my revolver?

HODSON. Revolver, sir! Yes sir. Mr Doyle uses it as a paperweight, sir, when he's drawing.

BROADBENT. Well, I want it packed. Theres a packet of cartridges somewhere, I think. Find it and pack it as well.

HODSON. Yes sir.

BROADBENT. By the way, pack your own traps too. I shall take you with me this time.

HODSON [*hesitant*] Is it a dangerous part youre going to, sir? Should I be expected to carry a revolver, sir?

BROADBENT. Perhaps it might be as well. I'm going to Ireland.

HODSON [*reassured*] Yes sir.

BROADBENT. You dont feel nervous about it, I suppose?

HODSON. Not at all, sir. I'll risk it, sir.

BROADBENT. Ever been in Ireland?

HODSON. No sir. I understand it's a very wet climate, sir. I'd better pack your india-rubber overalls.

BROADBENT. Do. Wheres Mr Doyle?

HODSON. I'm expecting him at five, sir. He went out after lunch.

BROADBENT. Anybody been looking for me?

HODSON. A person giving the name of Haffigan has called twice today, sir.

BROADBENT. Oh, I'm sorry. Why didnt he wait? I told him to wait if I wasnt in.

HODSON. Well sir, I didnt know you expected him; so I thought it best to — to — not to encourage him, sir.

BROADBENT. Oh, he's all right. He's an Irishman, and not very particular about his appearance.

HODSON. Yes sir: I noticed that he was rather Irish.

BROADBENT. If he calls again let him come up.

HODSON. I think I saw him waiting about, sir, when you drove up. Shall I fetch him, sir?

BROADBENT. Do, Hodson.

HODSON. Yes sir [*He makes for the outer door*].

BROADBENT. He'll want tea. Let us have some.

HODSON [*stopping*] I shouldnt think he drank tea, sir.

BROADBENT. Well, bring whatever you think he'd like.

HODSON. Yes sir [*An electric bell rings*]. Here he is, sir. Saw you arrive, sir.

BROADBENT. Right. Shew him in. [*Hodson goes out. Broadbent gets through the rest of his letters before Hodson returns with the visitor*].

HODSON. Mr Affigan.

Haffigan is a stunted, shortnecked, smallheaded man of about 30, with a small bullet head, a red nose, and furtive eyes. He is dressed in seedy black, almost clerically, and might be a tenth-rate schoolmaster ruined by drink. He hastens to shake Broadbent's hand with a show of reckless geniality and high spirits, helped out by a rollicking stage brogue. This is perhaps a comfort to himself, as he is secretly pursued by the horrors of incipient delirium tremens.

HAFFIGAN. Tim Haffigan, sir, at your service. The top o the mornin to you, Misther Broadbent.

BROADBENT [*delighted with his Irish visitor*] Good afternoon, Mr Haffigan.

TIM. An is it the afthernoon it is already? Begorra, what I call the mornin is all the time a man fasts afther breakfast.

BROADBENT. Havnt you lunched?

TIM. Divil a lunch!

BROADBENT. I'm sorry I couldnt get back from Brighton in time to offer you some; but —

TIM. Not a word, sir, not a word. Sure itll do tomorrow. Besides, I'm Irish, sir: a poor aither, but a powerful dhrinker.

BROADBENT. I was just about to ring for tea when you came. Sit down, Mr Haffigan.

TIM. Tay is a good dhrink if your nerves can stand it. Mine cant.

Haffigan sits down at the writing table, with his back to the filing cabinet. Broadbent sits opposite him. Hodson enters empty-handed; takes two glasses, a siphon, and a tantalus from the cupboard: places them before Broadbent on the writing table; looks ruthlessly at Haffigan, who cannot meet his eye; and retires.

BROADBENT. Try a whisky and soda.

TIM [*sobered*] There you touch the national wakeness, sir. [*Piously*] Not that I share it meself. Ive seen too much of the mischief of it.

BROADBENT [*pouring the whisky*] Say when.

TIM. Not too sthrong. [*Broadbent stops and looks inquiringly at him*]. Say half-an-half. [*Broadbent, somewhat startled by this demand, pours a little more, and again stops and looks*]. Just a dhrain more: the lower half o the tumber doesnt hold a fair half. Thankya.

BROADBENT [*laughing*] You Irishmen certainly know how to drink. [*Pouring some whisky for himself*] Now thats my poor English idea of a whisky and soda.

TIM. An a very good idea it is too. Dhrink is the curse o me unhappy counthry. I take it meself because Ive a wake heart and a poor digestion; but in principle I'm a teetoatler.

BROADBENT [*suddenly solemn and strenuous*] So am I, of course. I'm a Local Optionist to the backbone. You have no idea, Mr Haffigan, of the ruin that is wrought in this country by the unholy alliance of the publicans, the bishops, the Tories, and The Times. We must close the public-houses at all costs [*he drinks*].

TIM. Sure I know. It's awful [*he drinks*]. I see youre a good Liberal like meself, sir.

BROADBENT. I am a lover of liberty, like every true Englishman, Mr Haffigan. My name is Broadbent. If my name were Breitstein, and I had a hooked nose and a house in Park Lane, I should carry a Union Jack handkerchief and a penny trumpet, and tax the food of the people to support the Navy League, and clamor for the destruction of the last remnants of national liberty –

TIM. Not another word. Shake hands.

BROADBENT. But I should like to explain –

TIM. Sure I know every word youre goin to say before yev said it. *I* know the sort o man yar. An so youre thinkin o comin to Ireland for a bit?

BROADBENT. Where else can I go? I am an Englishman and a Liberal; and now that South Africa has been enslaved and destroyed, there is no country left to me to take an interest in but Ireland. Mind: I dont say that an Englishman has not other duties. He has a duty to Finland and a duty to Macedonia. But what sane man can deny that an Englishman's first duty is his duty to Ireland? Unfortunately, we have politicians here more unscrupulous than Bobrikoff, more bloodthirsty than Abdul the Damned; and it is under their heel that Ireland is now writhing.

TIM. Faith, theyve reckoned up with poor oul Bobrikoff anyhow.

BROADBENT. Not that I defend assassination: God forbid! However strongly we may feel that the unfortunate and patriotic young man who avenged the wrongs of Finland on the Russian tyrant was perfectly right from his own point of view, yet every civilized man must regard murder with abhorrence. Not even in defence of Free Trade would I lift my hand against a political opponent, however richly he might deserve it.

TIM. I'm sure you wouldnt; and I honor you for it. Youre goin to Ireland, then, out o sympithy: is it?

BROADBENT. I'm going to develop an estate there for the Land Development Syndicate, in which I am interested. I am convinced that all it needs to make it pay is to handle it properly, as estates are handled in England. You know the English plan, Mr Haffigan, dont you?

TIM. Bedad I do, sir. Take all you can out of Ireland and spend it in England: thats it.

BROADBENT [not quite liking this] My plan, sir, will be to take a little money out of England and spend it in Ireland.

TIM. More power to your elbow! an may your shadda never be less! for youre the broth of a boy entirely. An how can I help you? Command me to the last dhrop o me blood.

BROADBENT. Have you ever heard of Garden City?

TIM [doubtfully] D'ye mane heavn?

BROADBENT. Heaven! No: it's near Hitchin. If you can spare half an hour I'll go into it with you.

TIM. I tell you hwat. Gimme a prospectus. Lemmy take it home and reflect on it.

BROADBENT. Youre quite right: I will [He gives him a copy of Ebenezer Howard's book, and several pamphlets]. You understand that the map of the city – the circular construction – is only a suggestion.

TIM. I'll make a careful note o that [looking dazedly at the map].

BROADBENT. What I say is, why not start a Garden City in Ireland?

TIM [*with enthusiasm*] Thats just what was on the tip o me tongue to ask you. Why not? [*Defiantly*] Tell me why not.

BROADBENT. There are difficulties. I shall overcome them; but there are difficulties. When I first arrive in Ireland I shall be hated as an Englishman. As a Protestant, I shall be denounced from every altar. My life may be in danger. Well, I am prepared to face that.

TIM. Never fear, sir. We know how to respict a brave innimy.

BROADBENT. What I really dread is misunderstanding. I think you could help me to avoid that. When I heard you speak the other evening in Bermondsey at the meeting of the National League, I saw at once that you were – You wont mind my speaking frankly?

TIM. Tell me all me faults as man to man. I can stand anything but flatthery.

BROADBENT. May I put it in this way? that I saw at once that you are a thorough Irishman, with all the faults and all the qualities of your race: rash and improvident but brave and goodnatured; not likely to succeed in business on your own account perhaps, but eloquent, humorous, a lover of freedom, and a true follower of that great Englishman Gladstone.

TIM. Spare me blushes. I mustnt sit here to be praised to me face. But I confess to the goodnature: it's an Irish wakeness. I'd share me last shillin with a friend.

BROADBENT. I feel sure you would, Mr Haffigan.

TIM [*impulsively*] Damn it! call me Tim. A man that talks about Ireland as you do may call me anything. Gimmy a howlt o that whisky bottle [*he replenishes*].

BROADBENT [*smiling indulgently*] Well, Tim, will you come with me and help to break the ice between me and your warmhearted, impulsive countrymen?

TIM. Will I come to Madagascar or Cochin China wid you? Bedad I'll come to the North Pole wid you if yll pay me fare; for the divil a shillin I have to buy a third class ticket.

BROADBENT. Ive not forgotten that, Tim. We must put that little matter on a solid English footing, though the rest can be as Irish as you please. You must come as my – my – well, I hardly know what to call it. If we call you my agent, theyll shoot you. If we call you a bailiff, theyll duck you in the horsepond. I have a secretary already; and –

TIM. Then we'll call him the Home Secretary and me the Irish Secretary. Eh?

BROADBENT [*laughing industriously*] Capital. Your Irish wit has settled the first difficulty. Now about your salary —

TIM. A salary, is it? Sure I'd do it for nothin, only me cloes ud disgrace you; and I'd be dhriven to borra money from your friends: a thing thats agin me nacher. But I wont take a penny more than a hundherd a year. [*He looks with restless cunning at Broadbent, trying to guess how far he may go*].

BROADBENT. If that will satisfy you —

TIM [*more than reassured*] Why shouldnt it satisfy me? A hundherd a year is twelve pound a month, isnt it?

BROADBENT. No. Eight pound six and eightpence.

TIM. Oh murdher! An I'll have to sind five timmy poor oul mother in Ireland. But no matther: I said a hundherd; and what I said I'll stick to, if I have to starve for it.

BROADBENT [*with business caution*] Well, let us say twelve pounds for the first month. Afterwards, we shall see how we get on.

TIM. Youre a gentleman, sir. Whin me mother turns up her toes, you shall take the five pounds off; for your expinses must be kep down wid a sthrong hand; an — [*He is interrupted by the arrival of Broadbent's partner*].

Mr Laurence Doyle is a man of 36, with cold grey eyes, strained nose, fine fastidious lips, critical brows, clever head, rather refined and goodlooking on the whole, but with a suggestion of thinskinnedness and dissatisfaction that contrasts strongly with Broadbent's eupeptic jollity.

He comes in as a man at home there, but on seeing the stranger shrinks at once, and is about to withdraw when Broadbent reassures him. He then comes forward to the table, between the two others.

DOYLE [*retreating*] Youre engaged.

BROADBENT. Not at all, not at all. Come in. [*to Tim*] This gentleman is a friend who lives with me here: my partner, Mr Doyle. [*To Doyle*] This is a new Irish friend of mine, Mr Tim Haffigan.

TIM [*rising with effusion*] Sure it's meself thats proud to meet any friend o Misther Broadbent's. The top o the mornin to you, sir! Me heart goes out teeye both. It's not often I meet two such splendid speciments iv the Anglo-Saxon race.

BROADBENT [*chuckling*] Wrong for once, Tim. My friend Mr Doyle is a countryman of yours.

Tim is noticeably dashed by this announcement. He draws in his horns at once, and scowls suspiciously at Doyle under a vanishing mask of goodfellowship: cringing a little, too, in mere nerveless fear of him.

DOYLE [*with cool disgust*] Good evening. [*He retires to the fireplace, and says to Broadbent in a tone which conveys the strongest possible hint to Haffigan that he is unwelcome*] Will you soon be disengaged?

TIM [*his brogue decaying into a common would-be genteel accent with an unexpected strain of Glasgow in it*] I must be going. Avnmpoartnt engeegement in the west end.

BROADBENT [*rising*] It's settled, then, that you come with me.

TIM. Ashll be verra pleased to accompany ye, sir.

BROADBENT. But how soon? Can you start tonight? from Paddington? We go by Milford Haven.

TIM [*hesitating*] Well – A'm afraid – A [*Doyle goes abruptly into the bedroom, slamming the door and shattering the last remnant of Tim's nerve. The poor wretch saves himself from bursting into tears by plunging again into his role of daredevil Irishman. He rushes to Broadbent; plucks at his sleeve with trembling fingers; and pours forth his entreaty with all the brogue he can muster, subduing his voice lest Doyle should hear and return*]. Misther Broadbent: dont humiliate me before a fella counthryman. Look here: me cloes is up the spout. Gimmy a fypounnote – I'll pay ya nex Choosda whin me ship comes home – or you can stop it out o me month's sallery. I'll be on the platform at Paddnton punctial an ready. Gimmy it quick, before he comes back. You wont mind me axin, will ye?

BROADBENT. Not at all. I was about to offer you an advance for travelling expenses. [*He gives him a bank note*].

TIM [*pocketing it*] Thank you. I'll be there half an hour before the thrain starts. [*Larry is heard at the bedroom door, returning*]. Whisht: he's comin back. Goodbye and God bless ye. [*He hurries out almost crying, the £5 note and all the drink it means to him being too much for his empty stomach and overstrained nerves*].

DOYLE [*returning*] Where the devil did you pick up that seedy swindler? What was he doing here? [*He goes up to the table where the plans are, and makes a note on one of them, referring to his pocket book as he does so*].

BROADBENT. There you go! Why are you so down on every Irishman you meet, especially if he's a bit shabby? poor devil! Surely a fellow-countryman may pass you the top of the morning without offence, even if his coat is a bit shiny at the seams.

DOYLE [*contemptuously*] The top of the morning! Did he call you the broth of a boy? [*He comes to the writing table*].

BROADBENT [*triumphantly*] Yes.

DOYLE. And wished you more power to your elbow?

BROADBENT. He did.

DOYLE. And that your shadow might never be less?

BROADBENT. Certainly.

DOYLE [*taking up the depleted whisky bottle and shaking his head at it*] And he got about half a pint of whisky out of you.

BROADBENT. It did him no harm. He never turned a hair.

DOYLE. How much money did he borrow?

BROADBENT. It was not borrowing exactly. He shewed a very honorable spirit about money. I believe he would share his last shilling with a friend.

DOYLE. No doubt he would share his friend's last shilling if his friend was fool enough to let him. How much did he touch you for?

BROADBENT. Oh, nothing. An advance on his salary – for travelling expenses.

DOYLE. Salary! In Heaven's name, what for?

BROADBENT. For being my Home Secretary, as he very wittily called it.

DOYLE. I dont see the joke.

BROADBENT. You can spoil any joke by being cold blooded about it. I saw it all right when he said it. It was something – something really very amusing – about the Home Secretary and the Irish Secretary. At all events, he's evidently the very man to take with me to Ireland to break the ice for me. He can gain the confidence of the people there, and make them friendly to me. Eh? [*He seats himself on the office stool, and tilts it back so that the edge of the standing desk supports his back and prevents his toppling over*].

DOYLE. A nice introduction, by George! Do you suppose the whole population of Ireland consists of drunken begging letter writers, or that even if it did, they would accept one another as references?

BROADBENT. Pooh! nonsense! he's only an Irishman. Besides, you dont seriously suppose that Haffigan can humbug me, do you?

DOYLE. No: he's too lazy to take the trouble. All he has to do is to sit there and drink your whisky while you humbug yourself. However, we neednt argue about Haffigan, for two reasons. First, with your money in his pocket he will never reach Paddington: there are too many public houses on the way. Second, he's not an Irishman at all.

BROADBENT. Not an Irishman! [*He is so amazed by the statement that he straightens himself and brings the stool bolt upright*].

DOYLE. Born in Glasgow. Never was in Ireland in his life. I know all about him.

BROADBENT. But he spoke – he behaved just like an Irishman.

DOYLE. Like an Irishman!! Man alive, dont you know that all this top-o-the-morning and broth-of-a-boy and more-power-to-your-elbow business is got up in England to fool you, like the Albert Hall concerts of Irish music? No Irishman ever talks like that in Ireland, or ever did, or ever will. But when a thoroughly worthless Irishman comes to England, and finds the whole place full of romantic duffers like you, who will let him loaf and drink and sponge and brag as long as he flatters your sense of moral superiority by playing the fool and degrading himself and his country, he soon learns the antics that take you in. He picks them up at the theatre or the music hall. Haffigan learnt the rudiments from his father, who came from my part of Ireland. I knew his uncles, Matt and Andy Haffigan of Rosscullen.

BROADBENT [*still incredulous*] But his brogue?

DOYLE. His brogue! A fat lot you know about brogues! Ive heard you call a Dublin accent that you could hang your hat on, a brogue. Heaven help you! you dont know the difference between Connemara and Rathmines. [*With violent irritation*] Oh, damn Tim Haffigan! lets drop the subject: he's not worth wrangling about.

BROADBENT. Whats wrong with you today, Larry? Why are you so bitter? *Doyle looks at him perplexedly; comes slowly to the writing table; and sits down at the end next the fireplace before replying.*

DOYLE. Well: your letter completely upset me, for one thing.

BROADBENT. Why?

DOYLE. Your foreclosing this Rosscullen mortgage and turning poor Nick

Lestrange out of house and home has rather taken me aback; for I liked
the old rascal when I was a boy and had the run of his park to play in.
I was brought up on the property.

BROADBENT. But he wouldnt pay the interest. I had to foreclose on behalf
of the Syndicate. So now I'm off to Rosscullen to look after the property
myself. [*He sits down at the writing table opposite Larry, and adds,
casually, but with an anxious glance at his partner*] Youre coming with
me, of course?

DOYLE [*rising nervously and recommencing his restless movements*] Thats it.
Thats what I dread. Thats what has upset me.

BROADBENT. But dont you want to see your country again after 18 years
absence? to see your people? to be in the old home again? to –

DOYLE [*interrupting him very impatiently*] Yes, yes: I know all that as well
as you do.

BROADBENT. Oh well, of course [*with a shrug*] if you take it in that way, I'm
sorry.

DOYLE. Never you mind my temper: it's not meant for you, as you ought to
know by this time. [*He sits down again, a little ashamed of his petulance;
reflects a moment bitterly; then bursts out*] I have an instinct against going
back to Ireland: an instinct so strong that I'd rather go with you to the
South Pole than to Rosscullen.

BROADBENT. What! Here you are, belonging to a nation with the strongest
patriotism! the most inveterate homing instinct in the world! and you
pretend youd rather go anywhere than back to Ireland. You dont
suppose I believe you, do you? In your heart –

DOYLE. Never mind my heart: an Irishman's heart is nothing but his
imagination. How many of all those millions that have left Ireland have
ever come back or wanted to come back? But whats the use of talking
to you? Three verses of twaddle about the Irish emigrant 'sitting on the
stile, Mary', or three hours of Irish patriotism in Bermondsey or the
Scotland Division of Liverpool, go further with you than all the facts
that stare you in the face. Why, man alive, look at me! You know the
way I nag, and worry, and carp, and cavil, and disparage, and am never
satisfied and never quiet, and try the patience of my best friends.

BROADBENT. Oh, come, Larry! do yourself justice. Youre very amusing
and agreeable to strangers.

DOYLE. Yes, to strangers. Perhaps if I was a bit stiffer to strangers, and a bit easier at home, like an Englishman, I'd be better company for you.

BROADBENT. We get on well enough. Of course you have the melancholy of the Keltic race –

DOYLE [*bounding out of his chair*] Good God!!!

BROADBENT [*slyly*] – and also its habit of using strong language when theres nothing the matter.

DOYLE. Nothing the matter! When people talk about the Celtic race, I feel as if I could burn down London. That sort of rot does more harm than ten Coercion Acts. Do you suppose a man need be a Celt to feel melancholy in Rosscullen? Why, man, Ireland was peopled just as England was; and its breed was crossed by just the same invaders.

BROADBENT. True. All the capable people in Ireland are of English extraction. It has often struck me as a most remarkable circumstance that the only party in parliament which shews the genuine old English character and spirit is the Irish party. Look at its independence, its determination, its defiance of bad Governments, its sympathy with oppressed nationalities all the world over! How English!

DOYLE. Not to mention the solemnity with which it talks old fashioned nonsense which it knows perfectly well to be a century behind the times. Thats English, if you like.

BROADBENT. No, Larry, no. You are thinking of the modern hybrids that now monopolize England. Hypocrites, humbugs, Germans, Jews, Yankees, foreigners, Park Laners, cosmopolitan riffraff. Dont call them English. They dont belong to the dear old island, but to their confounded new empire; and by George! theyre worthy of it; and I wish them joy of it.

DOYLE [*unmoved by this outburst*] There! You feel better now, dont you?

BROADBENT [*defiantly*] I do. Much better.

DOYLE. My dear Tom, you only need a touch of the Irish climate to be as big a fool as I am myself. If all my Irish blood were poured into your veins, you wouldnt turn a hair of your constitution and character. Go and marry the most English Englishwoman you can find, and then bring up your son in Rosscullen; and that son's character will be so like mine and so unlike yours that everybody will accuse me of being the father. [*With sudden anguish*] Rosscullen! oh, good Lord, Rosscullen! The dullness! The hopelessness! the ignorance! the bigotry!

BROADBENT [*matter-of-factly*] The usual thing in the country, Larry. Just the same here.

DOYLE [*hastily*] No, no: the climate is different. Here, if the life is dull, you can be dull too, and no great harm done. [*Going off into a passionate dream*] But your wits cant thicken in that soft moist air, on those white springy roads, in those misty rushes and brown bogs, on those hillsides of granite rocks and magenta heather. Youve no such colors in the sky, no such lure in the distances, no such sadness in the evenings. Oh, the dreaming! the dreaming! the torturing, heart-scalding, never satisfying dreaming, dreaming, dreaming, dreaming! [*Savagely*] No debauchery that ever coarsened and brutalized an Englishman can take the worth and usefulness out of him like that dreaming. An Irishman's imagination never lets him alone, never convinces him, never satisfies him; but it makes him that he cant face reality nor deal with it nor handle it nor conquer it: he can only sneer at them that do, and [*bitterly, at Broadbent*] be 'agreeable to strangers', like a good-for-nothing woman on the streets. [*Gabbling at Broadbent across the table*] It's all dreaming, all imagination. He cant be religious. The inspired Churchman that teaches him the sanctity of life and the importance of conduct is sent away empty; while the poor village priest that gives him a miracle or a sentimental story of a saint, has cathedrals built for him out of the pennies of the poor. He cant be intelligently political: he dreams of what the Shan Van Vocht said in ninetyeight. If you want to interest him in Ireland youve got to call the unfortunate island Kathleen ni Hoolihan and pretend she's a little old woman. It saves thinking. It saves working. It saves everything except imagination, imagination, imagination; and imagination's such a torture that you cant bear it without whisky. [*With fierce shivering self-contempt*] At last you get that you can bear nothing real at all: youd rather starve than cook a meal; youd rather go shabby and dirty than set your mind to take care of your clothes and wash yourself; you nag and squabble at home because your wife isnt an angel, and she despises you because youre not a hero; and you hate the whole lot round you because theyre only poor slovenly useless devils like yourself. [*Dropping his voice like a man making some shameful confidence*] And all the while there goes on a horrible, senseless, mischievous laughter. When youre young, you exchange vile stories with them; and as youre too futile to be able to help or cheer them, you chaff and sneer and taunt them for not doing the things you darent do yourself. And all the time you laugh! laugh! laugh! eternal derision, eternal envy, eternal folly, eternal fouling and staining and degrading, until, when you come at last to a country where men take a question seriously and give a serious answer to it, you deride them for having no sense of humor, and plume yourself on your own worthlessness as if it made you better than them.

BROADBENT [*roused to intense earnestness by Doyle's eloquence*] Never despair, Larry. There are great possibilities for Ireland. Home Rule will work wonders under English guidance.

DOYLE [*pulled up short, his face twitching with a reluctant smile*] Tom: why do you select my most tragic moments for your most irresistible strokes of humor?

BROADBENT. Humor! I was perfectly serious. What do you mean? Do you doubt my seriousness about Home Rule?

DOYLE. I am sure you are serious, Tom, about the English guidance.

BROADBENT [*quite reassured*] Of course I am. Our guidance is the important thing. We English must place our capacity for government without stint at the service of nations who are less fortunately endowed in that respect; so as to allow them to develop in perfect freedom to the English level of self-government, you know. You understand me?

DOYLE. Perfectly. And Rosscullen will understand you too.

BROADBENT [*cheerfully*] Of course it will. So thats all right. [*He pulls up his chair and settles himself comfortably to lecture Doyle*]. Now Larry, Ive listened carefully to all youve said about Ireland; and I can see nothing whatever to prevent your coming with me. What does it all come to? Simply that you were only a young fellow when you were in Ireland. Youll find all that chaffing and drinking and not knowing what to be at in Peckham just the same as in Donnybrook. You looked at Ireland with a boy's eyes and saw only boyish things. Come back with me and look at it with a man's; and get a better opinion of your country.

DOYLE. I daresay youre partly right in that: at all events I know very well that if I had been the son of a laborer instead of the son of a country landagent, I should have struck more grit than I did. Unfortunately I'm not going back to visit the Irish nation, but to visit my father and Aunt Judy and Nora Reilly and Father Dempsey and the rest of them.

BROADBENT. Well, why not? Theyll be delighted to see you, now that England has made a man of you.

DOYLE [*struck by this*] Ah! you hit the mark there, Tom, with true British inspiration.

BROADBENT. Common sense, you mean.

DOYLE [*quickly*] No I dont: youve no more common sense than a gander. No Englishman has any common sense, or ever had, or ever will have. Youre going on a sentimental expedition for perfectly ridiculous reasons with your head full of political nonsense that would not take in any ordinarily intelligent donkey; but you can hit me in the eye with the simple truth about myself and my father.

BROADBENT [*amazed*] I never mentioned your father.

DOYLE [*not heeding the interruption*] There he is in Rosscullen, a landagent who's always been in a small way because he's a Catholic, and the landlords are mostly Protestants. What with land courts reducing rents and Land Purchase Acts turning big estates into little holdings, he'd be a beggar if he hadnt taken to collecting the new purchase instalments instead of the old rents. I doubt if he's been further from home than Athenmullet for twenty years. And here am I, made a man of, as you say, by England.

BROADBENT [*apologetically*] I assure you I never meant —

DOYLE. Oh, dont apologize: it's quite true. I daresay Ive learnt something in America and a few other remote and inferior spots; but in the main it is by living with you and working in double harness with you that I have learnt to live in a real world and not in an imaginary one. I owe more to you than to any Irishman.

BROADBENT [*shaking his head with a twinkle in his eye*] Very friendly of you, Larry, old man, but all blarney. I like blarney; but it's rot, all the same.

DOYLE. No it's not. I should never have done anything without you; though I never stop wondering at that blessed old head of yours with all its ideas in watertight compartments, and all the compartments warranted impervious to anything it doesnt suit you to understand.

BROADBENT [*invincible*] Unmitigated rot, Larry, I assure you.

DOYLE. Well, at any rate you will admit that all my friends are either Englishmen or men of the big world that belongs to the big Powers. All the serious part of my life has been lived in that atmosphere: all the serious part of my work has been done with men of that sort. Just think of me as I am now going back to Rosscullen! to that hell of littleness and monotony! How am I to get on with a little country landagent that ekes out his 5 per cent with a little farming and a scrap of house property in the nearest country town? What am I to say to him? What is he to say to me?

BROADBENT [*scandalized*] But youre father and son, man!

DOYLE. What difference does that make? What would you say if I proposed a visit to your father?

BROADBENT [*with filial rectitude*] I always made a point of going to see my father regularly until his mind gave way.

DOYLE [*concerned*] Has he gone mad? You never told me.

BROADBENT. He has joined the Tariff Reform League. He would never have done that if his mind had not been weakened. [*Beginning to declaim*] He has fallen a victim to the arts of a political charlatan who –

DOYLE [*interrupting him*] You mean that you keep clear of your father because he differs from you about Free Trade, and you dont want to quarrel with him. Well, think of me and my father! He's a Nationalist and a Separatist. I'm a metallurgical chemist turned civil engineer. Now whatever else metallurgical chemistry may be, it's not national. It's international. And my business and yours as civil engineers is to join countries, not to separate them. The one real political conviction that our business has rubbed into us is that frontiers are hindrances and flags confounded nuisances.

BROADBENT [*still smarting under Mr Chamberlain's economic heresy*] Only when there is a protective tariff –

DOYLE [*firmly*] Now look here, Tom: you want to get in a speech on Free Trade; and youre not going to do it: I wont stand it. My father wants to make St George's Channel a frontier and hoist a green flag on College Green; and I want to bring Galway within 3 hours of Colchester and 24 of New York. I want Ireland to be the brains and imagination of a big Commonwealth, not a Robinson Crusoe island. Then theres the religious difficulty. My Catholicism is the Catholicism of Charlemagne or Dante, qualified by a great deal of modern science and folklore which Father Dempsey would call the ravings of an Atheist. Well, my father's Catholicism is the Catholicism of Father Dempsey.

BROADBENT [*shrewdly*] I dont want to interrupt you, Larry; but you know this is all gammon. These differences exist in all families; but the members rub on together all right. [*Suddenly relapsing into portentousness*] Of course there are some questions which touch the very foundations of morals; and on these I grant you even the closest relationships cannot excuse any compromise or laxity. For instance –

DOYLE [*impatiently springing up and walking about*] For instance, Home Rule, South Africa, Free Trade, and putting the Church schools on the Education Rate. Well, I should differ from my father on every one of them, probably, just as I differ from you about them.

BROADBENT. Yes; but you are an Irishman; and these things are not serious to you as they are to an Englishman.

DOYLE. What! not even Home Rule!

BROADBENT [*steadfastly*] Not even Home Rule. We owe Home Rule not to the Irish, but to our English Gladstone. No, Larry: I cant help thinking that theres something behind all this.

DOYLE [*hotly*] What is there behind it? Do you think I'm humbugging you?

BROADBENT. Dont fly out, old chap. I only thought –

DOYLE. What did you think?

BROADBENT. Well, a moment ago I caught a name which is new to me: a Miss Nora Reilly, I think. [*Doyle stops dead and stares at him with something like awe*]. I dont wish to be impertinent, as you know, Larry; but are you sure she has nothing to do with your reluctance to come to Ireland with me?

DOYLE [*sitting down again, vanquished*] Thomas Broadbent: I surrender. The poor silly-clever Irishman takes off his hat to God's Englishman. The man who could in all seriousness make that recent remark of yours about Home Rule and Gladstone must be simply the champion idiot of all the world. Yet the man who could in the very next sentence sweep away all my special pleading and go straight to the heart of my motives must be a man of genius. But that the idiot and the genius should be the same man! how is that possible? [*Springing to his feet*] By Jove, I see it all now. I'll write an article about it, and send it to Nature.

BROADBENT [*staring at him*] What on earth –

DOYLE. It's quite simple. You know that a caterpillar –

BROADBENT. A caterpillar!!!

DOYLE. Yes, a caterpillar. Now give your mind to what I am going to say; for it's a new and important scientific theory of the English national character. A caterpillar –

BROADBENT. Look here, Larry: dont be an ass.

DOYLE [*insisting*] I say a caterpillar and I mean a caterpillar. Youll understand presently. A caterpillar [*Broadbent mutters a slight protest, but does not press it*] when it gets into a tree, instinctively makes itself look exactly like a leaf; so that both its enemies and its prey may mistake it for one and think it not worth bothering about.

BROADBENT. Whats that got to do with our English national character?

DOYLE. I'll tell you. The world is as full of fools as a tree is full of leaves. Well, the Englishman does what the caterpillar does. He instinctively makes himself look like a fool, and eats up all the real fools at his ease while his enemies let him alone and laugh at him for being a fool like the rest. Oh, nature is cunning! cunning! [*He sits down, lost in contemplation of his word-picture*].

BROADBENT [*with hearty admiration*] Now you know, Larry, that would never have occurred to me. You Irish people are amazingly clever. Of course it's all tommy rot; but it's so brilliant, you know! How the dickens do you think of such things! You really must write an article about it: they'll pay you something for it. If Nature wont have it, I can get it into Engineering for you: I know the editor.

DOYLE. Lets get back to business. I'd better tell you about Nora Reilly.

BROADBENT. No: never mind. I shouldnt have alluded to her.

DOYLE. I'd rather. Nora has a fortune.

BROADBENT [*keenly interested*] Eh? How much?

DOYLE. Forty per annum.

BROADBENT. Forty thousand?

DOYLE. No forty. Forty pounds.

BROADBENT [*much dashed*] Thats what you call a fortune in Rosscullen, is it?

DOYLE. A girl with a dowry of five pounds calls it a fortune in Rosscullen. Whats more, £40 a year is a fortune there; and Nora Reilly enjoys a good deal of social consideration as an heiress on the strength of it. It has helped my father's household through many a tight place. My father was her father's agent. She came on a visit to us when he died, and has lived with us ever since.

BROADBENT [*attentively, beginning to suspect Larry of misconduct with Nora, and resolving to get to the bottom of it*] Since when? I mean how old were you when she came?

DOYLE. I was seventeen. So was she: if she'd been older she'd have had more sense than to stay with us. We were together for 18 months before I went up to Dublin to study. When I went home for Christmas and Easter, she was there. I suppose it used to be something of an event for her; though of course I never thought of that then.

BROADBENT. Were you at all hard hit?

DOYLE. Not really. I had only two ideas at that time: first, to learn to do something; and then to get out of Ireland and have a chance of doing it. She didnt count. I was romantic about her, just as I was romantic about Byron's heroines or the old Round Tower of Rosscullen; but she didnt count any more than they did. Ive never crossed St George's Channel since for her sake – never even landed at Queenstown and come back to London through Ireland.

BROADBENT. But did you ever say anything that would justify her in waiting for you?

DOYLE. No, never. But she is waiting for me.

BROADBENT. How do you know?

DOYLE. She writes to me – on her birthday. She used to write on mine, and send me little things as presents; but I stopped that by pretending that it was no use when I was travelling, as they got lost in the foreign post-offices. [*He pronounces post-offices with the stress on offices, instead of on post*].

BROADBENT. You answer the letters?

DOYLE. Not very punctually. But they get acknowledged at one time or another.

BROADBENT. How do you feel when you see her handwriting?

DOYLE. Uneasy. I'd give £50 to escape a letter.

BROADBENT [*looking grave, and throwing himself back in his chair to intimate that the cross-examination is over, and the result very damaging to the witness*] Hm!

DOYLE. What d'ye mean by Hm!

BROADBENT. Of course I know that the moral code is different in Ireland. But in England it's not considered fair to trifle with a woman's affections.

DOYLE. You mean that an Englishman would get engaged to another woman and return Nora her letters and presents with a letter to say he was unworthy of her and wished her every happiness?

BROADBENT. Well, even that would set the poor girl's mind at rest.

DOYLE. Would it? I wonder! One thing I can tell you; and that is that Nora would wait until she died of old age sooner than ask my intentions or condescend to hint at the possibility of my having any. You dont know what Irish pride is. England may have knocked a good deal of it out of me; but she's never been in England; and if I had to choose between wounding that delicacy in her and hitting her in the face, I'd hit her in the face without a moment's hesitation.

BROADBENT [*who has been nursing his knee and reflecting, apparently rather agreeably*] You know, all this sounds rather interesting. Theres the Irish charm about it. Thats the worst of you: the Irish charm doesnt exist for you.

DOYLE. Oh yes it does. But it's the charm of a dream. Live in contact with dreams and you will get something of their charm: live in contact with facts and you will get something of their brutality. I wish I could find a country to live in where the facts were not brutal and the dreams not unreal.

BROADBENT [*changing his attitude and responding to Doyle's earnestness with deep conviction: his elbows on the table and his hands clenched*] Dont despair, Larry, old boy: things may look black; but there will be a great change after the next election.

DOYLE [*jumping up*] Oh, get out, you idiot!

BROADBENT [*rising also, not a bit snubbed*] Ha! Ha! you may laugh; but we shall see. However, dont let us argue about that. Come now! you ask my advice about Miss Reilly?

DOYLE [*reddening*] No I dont. Damn your advice! [*Softening*] Lets have it, all the same.

BROADBENT. Well, everything you tell me about her impresses me favorably. She seems to have the feelings of a lady; and though we must face the fact that in England her income would hardly maintain her in the lower middle class –

DOYLE [*interrupting*] Now look here, Tom. That reminds me. When you go to Ireland, just drop talking about the middle class and bragging of belonging to it. In Ireland youre either a gentleman or youre not. If you want to be particularly offensive to Nora, you can call her a Papist; but if you call her a middle-class woman, Heaven help you!

BROADBENT [*irrepressible*] Never fear. Youre all descended from the ancient kings: I know that. [*Complacently*] I'm not so tactless as you think, my boy. [*Earnest again*] I expect to find Miss Reilly a perfect lady; and I strongly advise you to come and have another look at her before you make up your mind about her. By the way, have you a photograph of her?

DOYLE. Her photographs stopped at twenty-five.

BROADBENT [*saddened*] Ah yes, I suppose so. [*With feeling, severely*] Larry: youve treated that poor girl disgracefully.

DOYLE. By George, if she only knew that two men were talking about her like this —!

BROADBENT. She wouldnt like it, would she? Of course not. We ought to be ashamed of ourselves, Larry. [*More and more carried away by his new fancy*]. You know, I have a sort of presentiment that Miss Reilly is a very superior woman.

DOYLE [*staring hard at him*] Oh! you have, have you?

BROADBENT. Yes I have. There is something very touching about the history of this beautiful girl.

DOYLE. Beau —! Oho! Heres a chance for Nora! and for me! [*Calling*] Hodson.

HODSON [*appearing at the bedroom door*] Did you call, sir?

DOYLE. Pack for me too. I'm going to Ireland with Mr Broadbent.

HODSON. Right sir. [*He retires into the bedroom*].

BROADBENT [*clapping Doyle on the shoulder*] Thank you, old chap. Thank you.

ACT II

Rosscullen. Westward a hillside of granite rock and heather slopes upward across the prospect from south to north. A huge stone stands on it in a naturally impossible place, as if it had been tossed up there by a giant. Over the brow, in the desolate valley beyond, is a round tower. A lonely white high road trending away westward past the tower loses itself at the foot of the far mountains. It is evening; and there are great breadths of silken green in the Irish sky. The sun is setting.

A man with the face of a young saint, yet with white hair and perhaps 50 years on his back, is standing near the stone in a trance of intense melancholy, looking over the hills as if by mere intensity of gaze he could pierce the glories of the sunset and see into the streets of heaven. He is dressed in black, and is rather more clerical in appearances than most English curates are nowadays; but he does not wear the collar and waistcoat of a parish priest. He is roused from his trance by the chirp of an insect from a tuft of grass in a crevice of the stone. His face relaxes; he turns quietly, and gravely takes off his hat to the tuft, addressing the insect in a brogue which is the jocular assumption of a gentleman and not the natural speech of a peasant.

THE MAN. An is that yourself, Misther Grasshopper? I hope I see you well this fine evenin.

THE GRASSHOPPER [*prompt and shrill in answer*] X.X.

THE MAN [*encouragingly*] Thats right. I suppose now youve come out to make yourself miserable be admyerin the sunset?

THE GRASSHOPPER [*sadly*] X.X.

THE MAN. Aye, youre a thrue Irish grasshopper.

THE GRASSHOPPER [*loudly*] X.X.X.

THE MAN. Three cheers for ould Ireland, is it? That helps you to face out the misery and the poverty and the torment, doesnt it?

THE GRASSHOPPER [*plaintively*] X.X.

THE MAN. Ah, it's no use, me poor little friend. If you could jump as far as a kangaroo you couldnt jump away from your own heart an its punishment. You can only look at Heaven from here: you cant reach it. There! [*pointing with his stick to the sunset*] thats the gate o glory, isnt it?

THE GRASSHOPPER [*assenting*] X.X.

THE MAN. Sure it's the wise grasshopper yar to know that. But tell me this, Misther Unworldly Wiseman: why does the sight of Heaven wring your heart an mine as the sight of holy wather wrings the heart o the divil? What wickedness have you done to bring that curse on you? Here! where are you jumpin to? Wheres your manners to go skyrocketing like that out o the box in the middle o your confession [*he threatens it with his stick*]?

THE GRASSHOPPER [*penitently*] X.

THE MAN. [*lowering the stick*] I accept your apology; but dont do it again. And now tell me one thing before I let you go home to bed. Which would you say this country was: hell or purgatory?

THE GRASSHOPPER. X.

THE MAN. Hell! Faith I'm afraid youre right. I wondher what you and me did when we were alive to get sent here.

THE GRASSHOPPER [*shrilly*] X.X.

THE MAN [*nodding*] Well, as you say, it's a delicate subject; and I wont press it on you. Now off widja.

THE GRASSHOPPER. X.X. [*It springs away*].

THE MAN [*waving his stick*] God speed you! [*He walks away past the stone towards the brow of the hill. Immediately a young laborer, his face distorted with terror, slips round from behind the stone*].

THE LABORER [*crossing himself repeatedly*] Oh glory be to God! glory be to God! Oh Holy Mother an all the saints! Oh murdher! murdher! [*Beside himself, calling*] Fadher Keegan! Fadher Keegan!

THE MAN [*turning*] Who's there? What's that? [*He comes back and finds the laborer, who clasps his knees*] Patsy Farrell! What are you doing here?

PATSY. Oh for the love o God dont lave me here wi dhe grasshopper. I hard it spakin to you. Dont let it do me any harm, Father darlint.

KEEGAN. Get up, you foolish man, get up. Are you afraid of a poor insect because I pretended it was talking to me?

PATSY. Oh, it was no pretendin, Fadher dear. Didnt it give three cheers n say it was a divil out o hell? Oh say youll see me safe home, Fadher; n put a blessin on me or somethin [*he moans with terror*].

KEEGAN. What were you doin there, Patsy, listnin? Were you spyin on me?

PATSY. No, Fadher: on me oath an soul I wasnt: I was waitn to meet

Masther Larry n carry his luggage from the car; n I fell asleep on the grass; n you woke me talking to the grasshopper; n I hard its wicked little voice. Oh, d'ye think I'll die before year's out, Fadher?

KEEGAN. For shame, Patsy! Is that your religion, to be afraid of a little deeshy grasshopper? Suppose it was a divil, what call have you to fear it? If I could ketch it, I'd make you take it home widja in your hat for a penance.

PATSY. Sure, if you wont let it harm me, I'm not afraid, your riverence. [*He gets up, a little reassured. He is a callow, flaxen polled, smoothfaced, downy chinned lad, fully grown but not yet fully filled out, with blue eyes and an instinctively acquired air of helplessness and silliness, indicating, not his real character, but a cunning developed by his constant dread of a hostile dominance, which he habitually tries to disarm and tempt into unmasking by pretending to be a much greater fool than he really is. Englishmen think him half-witted, which is exactly what he intends them to think. He is clad in corduroy trousers, unbuttoned waistcoat, and coarse blue striped shirt*].

KEEGAN [*admonitorily*] Patsy: what did I tell you about callin me Father Keegan an your reverence? What did Father Dempsey tell you about it?

PATSY. Yis, Fadher.

KEEGAN. Father!

PATSY [*desperately*] Arra, hwat am I to call you? Fadher Dempsey sez youre not a priest; n we all know youre not a man: n how do we know what ud happen to us if we shewed any disrespect to you? N sure they say wanse a priest always a priest.

KEEGAN [*sternly*] It's not for the like of you, Patsy, to go behind the instruction of your parish priest and set yourself up to judge whether your Church is right or wrong.

PATSY. Sure I know that, sir.

KEEGAN. The Church let me be its priest as long as it thought me fit for its work. When it took away my papers it meant you to know that I was only a poor madman, unfit and unworthy to take charge of the souls of the people.

PATSY. But wasnt it only because you knew more Latn than Father Dempsey that he was jealous of you?

KEEGAN [*scolding him to keep himself from smiling*] How dar you, Patsy

Farrell, put your own wicked little spites and foolishnesses into the heart of your priest? For two pins I'd tell him what you just said.

PATSY [*coaxing*] Sure you wouldnt –

KEEGAN. Wouldnt I? God forgive you! youre little better than a heathen.

PATSY. Deedn I am, Fadher: it's me bruddher the tinsmith in Dublin youre thinkin of. Sure he had to be a free-thinker when he larnt a thrade and went to live in the town.

KEEGAN. Well, he'll get to Heaven before you if youre not careful, Patsy. And now you listen to me, once and for all. Youll talk to me and pray for me by the name of Pether Keegan, so you will. And when youre angry and tempted to lift your hand agen the donkey or stamp your foot on the little grasshopper, remember that the donkey's Pether Keegan's brother, and the grasshopper Pether Keegan's friend. And when youre tempted to throw a stone at a sinner or a curse at a beggar, remember that Pether Keegan is a worse sinner and a worse beggar, and keep the stone and the curse for him the next time you meet him. Now say God bless you, Pether, to me before I go, just to practise you a bit.

PATSY. Sure it wouldnt be right, Fadher, I cant –

KEEGAN. Yes you can. Now out with it; or I'll put this stick into your hand an make you hit me with it.

PATSY [*throwing himself on his knees in an ecstasy of adoration*] Sure it's your blessin I want, Fadher Keegan. I'll have no luck widhout it.

KEEGAN [*shocked*] Get up out o that, man. Dont kneel to me: I'm not a saint.

PATSY [*with intense conviction*] Oh in throth yar, sir. [*The grasshopper chirps. Patsy, terrified, clutches at Keegan's hands*] Dont set it on me, Fadher: I'll do anythin you bid me.

KEEGAN [*pulling him up*] You bosthoon, you! Dont you see that it only whistled to tell me Miss Reilly's comin? There! Look at her and pull yourself together for shame. Off widja to the road: youll be late for the car if you dont make haste [*bustling him down the hill*]. I can see the dust of it in the gap already.

PATSY. The Lord save us! [*He goes down the hill towards the road like a haunted man*].

Nora Reilly comes down the hill. A slight weak woman in a pretty muslin print gown (her best), she is a figure commonplace enough to Irish eyes; but on the inhabitants of fatter-fed, (crowded, hustling and bustling modern countries she makes a very different impression. The absence of any symptoms of coarseness or hardness or appetite in her, her comparative delicacy of manner and sensibility of apprehension, her fine hands and frail figure, her novel accent, with the caressing plaintive Irish melody of her speech, give her a charm which is all the more effective because, being untravelled, she is unconscious of it, and never dreams of deliberately dramatizing and exploiting it, as the Irishwomen in England do. For Tom Broadbent therefore, an attractive woman, whom he would even call ethereal. To Larry Doyle, an everyday woman fit only for the eighteenth century, helpless, useless, almost sexless, an invalid without the excuse of disease, an incarnation of everything in Ireland that drove him out of it. These judgments have little value and no finality; but they are the judgments on which her fate hangs just at present. Keegan touches his hat to her: he does not take it off.

NORA. Mr Keegan: I want to speak to you a minute if you dont mind.

KEEGAN [*dropping the broad Irish vernacular of his speech to Patsy*] An hour if you like, Miss Reilly: youre always welcome. Shall we sit down?

NORA. Thank you. [*They sit on the heather. She is shy and anxious; but she comes to the point promptly because she can think of nothing else*]. They say you did a gradle o travelling at one time.

KEEGAN. Well, you see I'm not a Mnooth man [*he means that he was not a student at Maynooth College*]. When I was young I admired the older generation of priests that had been educated in Salamanca. So when I felt sure of my vocation I went to Salamanca. Then I walked from Salamanca to Rome, an sted in a monastery there for a year. My pilgrimage to Rome taught me that walking is a better way of travelling than the train; so I walked from Rome to the Sorbonne in Paris; and I wish I could have walked from Paris to Oxford; for I was very sick on the sea. After a year of Oxford I had to walk to Jerusalem to walk the Oxford feeling off me. From Jerusalem I came back to Patmos, and spent six months at the monastery of Mount Athos. From that I came to Ireland and settled down as a parish priest until I went mad.

NORA [*startled*] Oh dont say that.

KEEGAN. Why not? Dont you know the story? how I confessed a black man and gave him absolution? and how he put a spell on me and drove me mad?

NORA. How can you talk such nonsense about yourself? For shame!

KEEGAN. It's not nonsense at all: it's true – in a way. But never mind the black man. Now that you know what a travelled man I am, what can I do for you? [*She hesitates and plucks nervously at the heather. He stays her hand gently*]. Dear Miss Nora: dont pluck the little flower. If it was a pretty baby you wouldnt want to pull its head off and stick it in a vawse o water to look at. [*The grasshopper chirps: Keegan turns his head and addresses it in the vernacular*]. Be aisy, me son: she wont spoil the swingswong in your little three. [*To Nora, resuming his urbane style*] You see I'm quite cracked; but never mind: I'm harmless. Now what is it?

NORA [*embarrassed*] Oh, only idle curiosity. I wanted to know whether you found Ireland — I mean the country part of Ireland, of course — very small and backwardlike when you came back to it from Rome and Oxford and all the great cities.

KEEGAN. When I went to those great cities I saw wonders I had never seen in Ireland. But when I came back to Ireland I found all the wonders there waiting for me. You see they had been there all the time; but my eyes had never been opened to them. I did not know what my own house was like, because I had never been outside it.

NORA. D'ye think thats the same with everybody?

KEEGAN. With everybody who has eyes in his soul as well as in his head.

NORA. But really and truly now, werent the people rather disappointing? I should think the girls must have seemed rather coarse and dowdy after the foreign princesses and people? But I suppose a priest wouldnt notice that.

KEEGAN. It's a priest's business to notice everything. I wont tell you all I noticed about women; but I'll tell you this. The more a man knows, and the farther he travels, the more likely he is to marry a country girl afterwards.

NORA [*blushing with delight*] Youre joking, Mr Keegan: I'm sure yar.

KEEGAN. My way of joking is to tell the truth. It's the funniest joke in the world.

NORA [*incredulous*] Galong with you!

KEEGAN [*springing up actively*] Shall we go down to the road and meet the car? [*She gives him her hand and he helps her up*]. Patsy Farrell told me you were expecting young Doyle.

NORA [*tossing her chin up at once*] Oh, I'm not expecting him particularly. It's a wonder he's come back at all. After staying away eighteen years he can harly expect us to be very anxious to see him: can he now?

KEEGAN. Well, not anxious perhaps; but you will be curious to see how much he's changed in all these years.

NORA [*with a sudden bitter flush*] I suppose thats all that brings him back to look at us just to see how much weve changed. Well, he can wait and see me by candlelight: I didnt come out to meet him: I'm going to walk to the Round Tower [*going west across the hill*].

KEEGAN. You couldnt do better this fine evening. [*Gravely*] I'll tell him where youve gone. [*She turns as if to forbid him; but the deep understanding in his eyes makes that impossible; and she only looks at him earnestly and goes. He watches her disappear on the other side of the hill; then says*] Aye, he's come to torment you; and youre driven already to torment him. [*He shakes his head, and goes slowly away across the hill in the opposite direction, lost in thought*].

By this time the car has arrived, and dropped three of its passengers on the high road at the foot of the hill. It is a monster jaunting car, black and dilapidated, one of the last survivors of the public vehicles known to earlier generations as Beeyankiny cars, the Irish having laid violent tongues on the name of their projector, one Bianconi, an enterprising Italian. The three passengers are the parish priest, Father Dempsey; Cornelius Doyle, Larry's father; and Broadbent, all in overcoats and as stiff as only an Irish car could make them.

The priest, stout and fatherly, falls far short of that finest type of country-side pastor which represents the genius of priesthood; but he is equally far above the base type in which a strongminded unscrupulous peasant uses the Church to extort money, power, and privilege. He is a priest neither by vocation nor ambition, but because the life suits him. He has boundless authority over his flock, and taxes them stiffly enough to be a rich man. The old Protestant ascendency is now too broken to gall him. On the whole, an easygoing, amiable, even modest man as long as his dues are paid and his authority and dignity fully admitted.

Cornelius Doyle is an elder of the small wiry type, with a hardskinned, rather worried face, clean shaven except for sandy whiskers blanching into a lustreless pale yellow and quite white at the roots. His dress is that of a country-town man of business: that is, an oldish shooting suit, with elastic sided boots quite unconnected with shooting. Feeling shy with Broadbent, he is hasty, which is his way of trying to appear genial.

Broadbent, for reasons which will appear later, has no luggage except a field glass and a guide book. The other two have left theirs to the unfortunate Patsy Farrell, who struggles up the hill after them, loaded with a sack of potatoes, a hamper, a fat goose, a colossal salmon, and several paper parcels.

Cornelius leads the way up the hill, with Broadbent at his heels. The priest follows. Patsy lags laboriously behind.

CORNELIUS. This is a bit of a climb, Mr Broadbent; but it's shorter than goin round be the road.

BROADBENT [*stopping to examine the great stone*] Just a moment, Mr Doyle: I want to look at this stone. It must be Finian's die-cast.

CORNELIUS [*in blank bewilderment*] Hwat?

BROADBENT. Murray describes it. One of your great national heroes – I cant pronounce the name – Finian Somebody, I think.

FATHER DEMPSEY [*also perplexed, and rather scandalized*] Is it Fin McCool you mean?

BROADBENT. I daresay it is. [*Referring to the guide book*] Murray says that a huge stone, probably of Druidic origin, is still pointed out as the die cast by Fin in his celebrated match with the devil.

CORNELIUS [*dubiously*] Jeuce a word I ever heard of it!

FATHER DEMPSEY [*very seriously indeed, and even a little severely*] Dont believe any such nonsense, sir. There never was any such thing. When people talk to you about Fin McCool and the like, take no notice of them. It's all idle stories and superstition.

BROADBENT [*somewhat indignantly; for to be rebuked by an Irish priest for superstition is more than he can stand*] You dont suppose I believe it, do you?

FATHER DEMPSEY. Oh, I thought you did. D'ye see the top of the Roun Tower there? thats an antiquity worth lookin at.

BROADBENT [*deeply interested*] Have you any theory as to what the Round Towers were for?

FATHER DEMPSEY [*a little offended*] A theory? Me! [*Theories are connected in his mind with the late Professor Tyndall, and with scientific scepticism generally: also perhaps with the view that the Round Towers are phallic symbols*].

CORNELIUS [*remonstrating*] Father Dempsey is the priest of the parish, Mr Broadbent. What would he be doing with a theory?

FATHER DEMPSEY [*with gentle emphasis*] I have a knowledge of what the Round Towers were, if thats what you mean. They are the fore-fingers of the early Church, pointing us all to God.

Patsy, intolerably overburdened, loses his balance, and sits down involuntarily. His burdens are scattered over the hillside. Cornelius and Father Dempsey turn furiously on him, leaving Broadbent beaming at the stone and the tower with fatuous interest.

CORNELIUS. Oh, be the hokey, the sammin's broke in two! You schoopid ass, what d'ye mean?

FATHER DEMPSEY. Are you drunk, Patsy Farrell? Did I tell you to carry that hamper carefully or did I not?

PATSY [*rubbing the back of his head, which has almost dinted a slab of granite*] Sure me fut slipt. Howkn I carry three men's luggage at wanst?

FATHER DEMPSEY. You were told to leave behind what you couldnt carry, an go back for it.

PATSY. An whose things was I to lave behind? Hwat would your reverence think if I left your hamper behind in the wet grass; n hwat would the masther say if I left the sammin and the goose be the side o the road for annywan to pick up?

CORNELIUS. Oh, youve a dale to say for yourself, you butther-fingered omadhaun. Waitll Ant Judy sees the state o that sammin: she'll talk to you. Here! gimmy that birdn that fish there; an take Father Dempsey's hamper to his house for him; n then come back for the rest.

FATHER DEMPSEY. Do, Patsy. And mind you dont fall down again.

PATSY. Sure I –

CORNELIUS [*bustling him up the hill*] Whisht! heres Ant Judy. [*Patsy goes grumbling in disgrace, with Father Dempsey's hamper*].

Aunt Judy comes down the hill, a woman of 50, in no way remarkable, lively and busy without energy or grip, placid without tranquillity, kindly without concern for others: indeed without much concern for herself: a contented product of a narrow, strainless life. She wears her hair parted in the middle and quite smooth, with a flattened bun at the back. Her dress is a plain brown frock, with a woollen pelerine of black and aniline mauve over her shoulders, all very trim in honor of the occasion. She looks round for Larry; is puzzled; then stares incredulously at Broadbent.

AUNT JUDY. Surely to goodness thats not you, Larry!

CORNELIUS. Arra how could he be Larry, woman alive? Larry's in no hurry home, it seems. I havnt set eyes on him. This is his friend, Mr Broadbent. Mr Broadbent: me sister Judy.

AUNT JUDY [*hospitably: going to Broadbent and shaking hands heartily*] Mr Broadbent! Fancy me takin you for Larry! Sure we havn't seen a sight of him for eighteen years, n he ony a lad when he left us.

BROADBENT. It's not Larry's fault: he was to have been here before me. He started in our motor an hour before Mr Doyle arrived, to meet us at Athenmullet, intending to get here long before me.

AUNT JUDY. Lord save us! do you think he's had n axidnt?

BROADBENT. No: he's wired to say he's had a breakdown and will come on as soon as he can. He expects to be here at about ten.

AUNT JUDY. There now! Fancy him trustn himself in a motor and we all expectn him! Just like him! he'd never do anything like anybody else. Well, what cant be cured must be injoored. Come on in, all of you. You must be dyin for your tea, Mr Broadbent.

BROADBENT [*with a slight start*] Oh, I'm afraid it's too late for tea [*he looks at his watch*].

AUNT JUDY. Not a bit: we never have it airlier than this. I hope they gave you a good dinner at Athenmullet.

BROADBENT [*trying to conceal his consternation as he realizes that he is not going to get any dinner after his drive*] Oh – er – excellent, excellent. By the way, hadnt I better see about a room at the hotel? [*They stare at him*].

CORNELIUS. The hotel!

FATHER DEMPSEY. Hwat hotel?

AUNT JUDY. Indeedn youre not going to a hotel. Youll stay with us. I'd have put you into Larry's room, ony the boy's pallyass is too short for you; but we'll make a comfortable bed for you on the sofa in the parlor.

BROADBENT. Youre very kind, Miss Doyle; but really I'm ashamed to give you so much trouble unnecessarily. I shant mind the hotel in the least.

FATHER DEMPSEY. Man alive! theres no hotel in Rosscullen.

BROADBENT. No hotel! Why, the driver told me there was the finest hotel in Ireland here. [*They regard him joylessly*].

AUNT JUDY. Arra would you mind what the like of him would tell you? Sure he'd say hwatever was the least trouble to himself and the pleasantest to you, thinkin you might give him a thruppeny bit for himself or the like.

BROADBENT. Perhaps theres a public house.

FATHER DEMPSEY [*grimly*] Theres seventeen.

AUNT JUDY. Ah then, how could you stay at a public house? theyd have no place to put you even if it was a right place for you to go. Come! is it the sofa youre afraid of? If it is, you can have me own bed. I can sleep with Nora.

BROADBENT. Not at all: I should be only too delighted. But to upset your arrangements in this way —

CORNELIUS [*anxious to cut short the discussion, which makes him ashamed of his house; for he guesses Broadbent's standard of comfort a little more accurately than his sister does*] Thats all right; itll be no trouble at all. Hweres Nora?

AUNT JUDY. Oh, how do I know? She slipped out a little while ago: I thought she was going to meet the car.

CORNELIUS [*dissatisfied*] It's a queer thing of her to run out o the way at such a time.

AUNT JUDY. Sure she's a queer girl altogether. Come. Come in: come in.

FATHER DEMPSEY. I'll say good night, Mr Broadbent. If theres anything I can do for you in this parish, let me know. [*He shakes hands with Broadbent*].

BROADBENT [*effusively cordial*] Thank you, Father Dempsey. Delighted to have met you, sir.

FATHER DEMPSEY [*passing on to Aunt Judy*] Good night, Miss Doyle.

AUNT JUDY. Wont you stay to tea?

FATHER DEMPSEY. Not tonight, thank you kindly: I have business to do at home. [*He turns to go, and meets Patsy Farrell returning unloaded*]. Have you left that hamper for me?

PATSY. Yis, your reverence.

FATHER DEMPSEY. Thats a good lad [*going*].

PATSY [*to Aunt Judy*] Fadher Keegan sez —

FATHER DEMPSEY [*turning sharply on him*] Whats that you say?

PATSY [*frightened*] Fadher Keegan —

FATHER DEMPSEY. How often have you heard me bid you call Mister Keegan in his proper name, the same as I do? Father Keegan indeed! Cant you tell the difference between your priest and any ole madman in a black coat?

PATSY. Sure I'm afraid he might put a spell on me.

FATHER DEMPSEY [*wrathfully*] You mind what I tell you or I'll put a spell on you thatll make you lep. D'ye mind that now? [*He goes home*].

Patsy goes down the hill to retrieve the fish, the bird, and the sack.

AUNT JUDY. Ah, hwy cant you hold your tongue, Patsy, before Father Dempsey?

PATSY. Well, hwat was I to do? Father Keegan bid me tell you Miss Nora was gone to the Roun Tower.

AUNT JUDY. An hwy couldnt you wait to tell us until Father Dempsey was gone?

PATSY. I was afeerd o forgetn it; and then may be he'd a sent the grasshopper or the little dark looker into me at night to remind me of it. [*The dark looker is the common grey lizard, which is supposed to walk down the throats of incautious sleepers and cause them to perish in a slow decline*].

CORNELIUS. Yah, you great gaum, you! Widjer grasshoppers and dark lookers! Here: take up them things and let me hear no more o your foolish lip. [*Patsy obeys*]. You can take the sammin under your oxther. [*He wedges the salmon into Patsy's axilla*].

PATSY. I can take the goose too, sir. Put it on me back n gimmy the neck of it in me mouth. [*Cornelius is about to comply thoughtlessly*].

AUNT JUDY [*feeling that Broadbent's presence demands special punctiliousness*] For shame, Patsy! to offer to take the goose in your mouth that we have to eat after you! The masterll bring it in for you.

PATSY. Arra what would a dead goose care for me mouth? [*He takes his load up the hill*].

CORNELIUS. Hwats Nora doin at the Roun Tower?

AUNT JUDY. Oh, the Lord knows! Romancin, I suppose. Praps she thinks Larry would go there to look for her and see her safe home.

BROADBENT. Miss Reilly must not be left to wait and walk home alone at night. Shall I go for her?

AUNT JUDY [*contemptuously*] Arra hwat ud happen to her? Hurry in now, Corny. Come, Mr Broadbent: I left the tea on the hob to draw; and itll be black if we dont go in and drink it.

They go up the hill. It is dusk by this time.

Broadbent does not fare so badly after all at Aunt Judy's board. He gets not only tea and bread-and-butter, but more mutton chops than he has ever conceived it possible to eat at one sitting. There is also a most filling substance called potato cake. Hardly have his fears of being starved been replaced by his first misgiving that he is eating too much and will be sorry for it tomorrow, when his appetite is revived by the production of a bottle of illicitly distilled whisky, called potcheen, which he has read and dreamed of (he calls it pottine) and is now at last to taste. His goodhumor rises almost to excitement before Cornelius shows signs of sleepiness. The contrast between Aunt Judy's table service and that of the south and east coast hotels at which he spends his Fridays-to-Tuesdays when he is in London, seems to him delightfully Irish. The almost total atrophy of any sense of enjoyment in Cornelius, or even any desire for it or toleration of the possibility of life being something better than a round of sordid worries, relieved by tobacco, punch, fine mornings, and petty successes in buying and selling, passes with his guest as the whimsical affectation of a shrewd Irish humorist and incorrigible spendthrift. Aunt Judy seems to him an incarnate joke. The likelihood that the joke will pall after a month or so, and is probably not apparent at any time to born Rossculleners, or that he himself unconsciously entertains Aunt Judy by his fantastic English personality and English mispronunciations, does not occur to him for a moment. In the end he is so charmed, and so loth to go to bed and perhaps dream of prosaic England, that he insists on going out to smoke a cigar and look for Nora Reilly at the Round Tower. Not that any special insistence is needed; for the English inhibitive instinct does not seem to exist in Rosscullen. Just as Nora's liking to miss a meal and stay out at the Round Tower is accepted as a sufficient reason for her doing it, and for the family going to bed and leaving the door open for her, so Broadbent's whim to go out for a late stroll provokes neither hospitable remonstrance nor surprise. Indeed Aunt Judy wants to get rid of him whilst she makes a bed for him on the sofa. So off he goes, full fed, happy and enthusiastic, to explore the valley by moonlight.

The Round Tower stands about half an Irish mile from Rosscullen, some fifty yards south of the road on a knoll with a circle of wild greensward on it. The road once ran over this knoll; but modern engineering has tempered the level to the Beeyankiny car by carrying the road partly round the knoll and partly through a cutting; so that the way from the road to the tower is a footpath up the embankment through furze and brambles.

On the edge of this slope, at the top of the path, Nora is straining her eyes in the moonlight, watching for Larry. At last she gives it up with a sob of impatience, and retreats to the hoary foot of the tower, where she sits down discouraged and cries a little. Then she settles herself resignedly to wait, and hums a song — not an Irish melody, but a hackneyed English drawing room ballad of the season before last — until some slight noise suggests a footstep, when she springs up eagerly and runs to the edge of the slope again. Some moments of silence and suspense follow, broken by unmistakable footsteps. She gives a little gasp as she sees a man approaching.

NORA. Is that you, Larry? [*Frightened a little*] Who's that?

BROADBENT'S *voice from below her on the path*. Dont be alarmed.

NORA. Oh, what an English accent youve got!

BROADBENT [*rising into view*] I must introduce myself —

NORA [*violently startled, retreating*] It's not you! Who are you? What do you want?

BROADBENT [*Advancing*] I'm really so sorry to have alarmed you, Miss Reilly. My name is Broadbent. Larry's friend, you know.

NORA [*chilled*] And has Mr Doyle not come with you?

BROADBENT. No. Ive come instead. I hope I am not unwelcome.

NORA [*deeply mortified*] I'm sorry Mr Doyle should have given you the trouble, I'm sure.

BROADBENT. You see, as a stranger and an Englishman, I thought it would be interesting to see the Round Tower by moonlight.

NORA. Oh, you came to see the tower. I thought — [*confused, trying to recover her manners*] Oh, of course. I was so startled. It's a beautiful night, isnt it?

BROADBENT. Lovely. I must explain why Larry has not come himself.

NORA. Why should he come? He's seen the tower often enough: it's no attraction to him [*Genteelly*] An what do you think of Ireland, Mr Broadbent? Have you ever been here before?

BROADBENT. Never.

NORA. An how do you like it?

BROADBENT [*suddenly betraying a condition of extreme sentimentality*] I can hardly trust myself to say how much I like it. The magic of this Irish scene, and — I really dont want to be personal, Miss Reilly; but the charm of your Irish voice —

NORA [*quite accustomed to gallantry, and attaching no seriousness whatever to it*] Oh, get along with you, Mr Broadbent! Youre breaking your heart about me already, I daresay, after seeing me for two minutes in the dark.

BROADBENT. The voice is just as beautiful in the dark you know. Besides, Ive heard a great deal about you from Larry.

NORA [*with bitter indifference*] Have you now? Well, thats a great honor, I'm sure.

BROADBENT. I have looked forward to meeting you more than to anything else in Ireland.

NORA [*ironically*] Dear me! did you now?

BROADBENT. I did really. I wish you had taken half as much interest in me.

NORA. Oh, I was dying to see you, of course. I daresay you can imagine the sensation an Englishman like you would make among us poor Irish people.

BROADBENT. Ah, now youre chaffing me, Miss Reilly: you know you are. You mustnt chaff me. I'm very much in earnest about Ireland and everything Irish. I'm very much in earnest about you and about Larry.

NORA. Larry has nothing to do with me, Mr Broadbent.

BROADBENT. If I really thought that, Miss Reilly, I should – well, I should let myself feel that charm of which I spoke just now more deeply than I – than I –

NORA. Is it making love to me you are?

BROADBENT [*scared and much upset*] On my word I believe I am, Miss Reilly. If you say that to me again I shant answer for myself: all the harps of Ireland are in your voice. [*She laughs at him. He suddenly loses his head and seizes her arms, to her great indignation*]. Stop laughing: do you hear? I am in earnest: in English earnest. When I say a thing like that to a woman, I mean it. [*Releasing her and trying to recover his ordinary manner in spite of his bewildering emotion*] I beg your pardon.

NORA. How dare you touch me?

BROADBENT. There are not many things I would not dare for you. That does not sound right perhaps; but I really – [*he stops and passes his hand over his forehead, rather lost*].

NORA. I think you ought to be ashamed. I think if you were a gentleman, and me alone with you in this place at night, you would die rather than do such a thing.

BROADBENT. You mean that it's an act of treachery to Larry?

NORA. Deed I dont. What has Larry to do with it? It's an act of disrespect and rudeness to me: it shews what you take me for. You can go your way now; and I'll go mine. Good night, Mr Broadbent.

BROADBENT. No, please, Miss Reilly. One moment. Listen to me. I'm serious: I'm desperately serious. Tell me that I'm interfering with

Larry; and I'll go straight from this spot back to London and never see you again. Thats on my honor: I will. Am I interfering with him?

NORA [*answering in spite of herself in a sudden spring of bitterness*] I should think you ought to know better than me whether youre interfering with him. Youve seen him oftener than I have. You know him better than I do, by this time. Youve come to me quicker than he has, havnt you?

BROADBENT. I'm bound to tell you, Miss Reilly, that Larry has not arrived in Rosscullen yet. He meant to get here before me; but his car broke down; and he may not arrive until tomorrow.

NORA [*her face lighting up*] Is that the truth?

BROADBENT. Yes: thats the truth. [*She gives a sigh of relief*]. Youre glad of that?

NORA [*up in arms at once*] Glad indeed! Why should I be glad? As weve waited eighteen years for him we can afford to wait a day longer, I should think.

BROADBENT. If you really feel like that about him, there may be a chance for another man yet. Eh?

NORA [*deeply offended*] I suppose people are different in England, Mr Broadbent; so perhaps you dont mean any harm. In Ireland nobody'd mind what a man'd say in fun, nor take advantage of what a woman might say in answer to it. If a woman couldnt talk to a man for two minutes at their first meeting without being treated the way youre treating me, no decent woman would ever talk to a man at all.

BROADBENT. I dont understand that. I dont admit that. I am sincere; and my intentions are perfectly honorable. I think you will accept the fact that I'm an Englishman as a guarantee that I am not a man to act hastily or romantically; though I confess that your voice had such an extraordinary effect on me just now when you asked me so quaintly whether I was making love to you –

NORA [*flushing*] I never thought –

BROADBENT [*quickly*] Of course you didnt: I'm not so stupid as that. But I couldnt bear your laughing at the feeling it gave me. You – [*again struggling with a surge of emotion*] you dont know what I – [*he chokes for a moment and then blurts out with unnatural steadiness*] Will you be my wife?

NORA [*promptly*] Deed I wont. The idea! [*Looking at him more carefully*] Arra, come home, Mr Broadbent; and get your senses back again. I think youre not accustomed to potcheen punch in the evening after your tea.

BROADBENT [*horrified*] Do you mean to say that I – I – I – my God! that I appear drunk to you, Miss Reilly?

NORA [*compassionately*] How many tumblers had you?

BROADBENT [*helplessly*] Two.

NORA. The flavor of the turf prevented you noticing the strength of it. Youd better come home to bed.

BROADBENT [*fearfully agitated*] But this is such a horrible doubt to put into my mind – to – to – For Heaven's sake, Miss Reilly, am I really drunk?

NORA [*soothingly*] Youll be able to judge better in the morning. Come on now back with me, an think no more about it. [*She takes his arm with motherly solicitude and urges him gently towards the path*].

BROADBENT [*yielding in despair*] I must be drunk: frightfully drunk; for your voice drove me out of my senses – [*he stumbles over a stone*]. No: on my word, on my most sacred word of honor, Miss Reilly, I tripped over that stone. It was an accident: it was indeed.

NORA. Yes, of course it was. Just take my arm, Mr Broadbent, while we're going down the path to the road. Youll be all right then.

BROADBENT [*submissively taking it*] I cant sufficiently apologize, Miss Reilly, or express my sense of your kindness when I am in such a disgusting state. How could I be such a bea – [*he trips again*] damn the heather! my foot caught in it.

NORA. Steady now, steady. Come along: come. [*He is led down to the road in the character of a convicted drunkard. To him there is something divine in the sympathetic indulgence she substitutes for the angry disgust with which one of his own countrywomen would resent his supposed condition. And he has no suspicion of the fact, or of her ignorance of it, that when an Englishman is sentimental he behaves very much as an Irishman does when he is drunk*].

ACT III

Next morning Broadbent and Larry are sitting at the ends of a breakfast table in the middle of a small grass plot before Cornelius Doyle's house. They have finished their meal, and are buried in newspapers. Most of the crockery is crowded upon a large square black tray of japanned metal. The teapot is of brown delft ware. There is no silver; and the butter, on a dinner plate, is en bloc. The background to this breakfast is the house, a small white slated building, accessible by a half-glazed door. A person coming out into the garden by this door would find the table straight in front of him, and a gate leading to the road half-way down the garden on his right; or, if he turned sharp to his left, he could pass round the end of the house through an unkempt shrubbery. The mutilated remnant of a huge plaster statue, nearly dissolved by the rains of a century, and vaguely resembling a majestic female in Roman draperies, with a wreath in her hand, stands neglected amid the laurels. Such statues, though apparently works of art, grow naturally in Irish gardens. Their germination is a mystery to the oldest inhabitants, to whose means and tastes they are totally foreign.

There is a rustic bench, much soiled by the birds, and decorticated and split by the weather, near the little gate. At the opposite side, a basket lies unmolested because it might as well be there as anywhere else. An empty chair at the table was lately occupied by Cornelius, who has finished his breakfast and gone into the room in which he receives rents and keeps his books and cash, known in the household as 'the office'. This chair, like the two occupied by Larry and Broadbent, has a mahogany frame and is upholstered in black horsehair.

Larry rises and goes off through the shrubbery with his newspaper. Hodson comes in through the garden gate, disconsolate. Broadbent, who sits facing the gate, augurs the worst from his expression.

BROADBENT. Have you been to the village?

HODSON. No use, sir. We'll have to get everything from London by parcel post.

BROADBENT. I hope they made you comfortable last night.

HODSON. I was no worse than you were on that sofa, sir. One expects to rough it here, sir.

BROADBENT. We shall have to look out for some other arrangement. [*Cheering up irrepressibly*] Still, it's no end of a joke. How do you like the Irish, Hodson?

HODSON. Well, sir, theyre all right anywhere but in their own country. Ive known lots of em in England, and generally liked em. But here, sir, I seem simply to hate em. The feeling come over me the moment we landed at Cork, sir. It's no use my pretendin, sir: I cant bear em. My mind rises up agin their ways, somehow: they rub me the wrong way all over.

BROADBENT. Oh, their faults are on the surface: at heart they are one of the finest races on earth. [*Hodson turns away, without affecting to respond to his enthusiasm*]. By the way, Hodson —

HODSON [*turning*] Yes, sir.

BROADBENT. Did you notice anything about me last night when I came in with that lady?

HODSON [*surprised*] No, sir.

BROADBENT. Not any — er —? You may speak frankly.

HODSON. I didnt notice nothing, sir. What sort of thing did you mean, sir?

BROADBENT. Well — er — er — well, to put it plainly, was I drunk?

HODSON [*amazed*] No, sir.

BROADBENT. Quite sure?

HODSON. Well, I should a said rather the opposite, sir. Usually when youve been enjoying yourself, youre a bit hearty like. Last night you seemed rather low, if anything.

BROADBENT. I certainly have no headache. Did you try the pottine, Hodson?

HODSON. I just took a mouthful, sir. It tasted of peat: oh! something horrid, sir. The people here call peat turf. Potcheen and strong porter is what they like, sir. I'm sure I dont know how they can stand it. Give me beer, I say.

BROADBENT. By the way, you told me I couldnt have porridge for break-fast; but Mr Doyle had some.

HODSON. Yes, sir. Very sorry, sir. They call it stirabout, sir: thats how it was. They know no better, sir.

BROADBENT. All right: I'll have some tomorrow.

Hodson goes to the house. When he opens the door he finds Nora and Aunt Judy on the threshold. He stands aside to let them pass, with the air of a well trained servant oppressed by heavy trials. Then he goes in. Broadbent rises. Aunt Judy goes to the table and collects the plates and cups on the tray. Nora goes to the back of the rustic seat and looks out at the gate with the air of a woman accustomed to have nothing to do. Larry returns from the shrubbery.

BROADBENT. Good morning, Miss Doyle.

AUNT JUDY [*thinking it absurdly late in the day for such a salutation*] Oh, good morning. [*Before moving his plate*] Have you done?

BROADBENT. Quite, thank you. You must excuse us for not waiting for you. The country air tempted us to get up early.

AUNT JUDY. N d'ye call this airly, God help you?

LARRY. Aunt Judy probably breakfasted about half past six.

AUNT JUDY. Whisht, you! draggin the parlor chairs out into the gardn n giving Mr Broadbent his death over his meals out here in the cold air. [*To Broadbent*] Why d'ye put up with his foolishness, Mr Broadbent?

BROADBENT. I assure you I like the open air.

AUNT JUDY. Ah galong! How can you like whats not natural? I hope you slept well.

NORA. Did anything wake yup with a thump at three o'clock? I thought the house was falling. But then I'm a very light sleeper.

LARRY. I seem to recollect that one of the legs of the sofa in the parlor had a way of coming out unexpectedly eighteen years ago. Was that it, Tom?

BROADBENT [*hastily*] Oh, it doesnt matter: I was not hurt — at least — er —

AUNT JUDY. Oh now what a shame! An I told Patsy Farrll to put a nail in it.

BROADBENT. He did, Miss Doyle. There was a nail, certainly.

AUNT JUDY. Dear oh dear!

An oldish peasant farmer, small, leathery, peat-faced, with a deep voice and a surliness that is meant to be aggressive, and is in effect pathetic — the voice of a man of hard life and many sorrows — comes in at the gate. He is old enough to have perhaps worn a long tailed frieze coat and knee breeches in his time; but now he is dressed respectably in a black frock coat, tall hat, and pollard colored trousers; and his face is as clean as washing can make it, though that is not saying much, as the habit is recently acquired and not yet congenial.

THE NEW-COMER [*at the gate*] God save all here! [*He comes a little way into the garden*].

LARRY [*patronizingly, speaking across the garden to him*] Is that yourself, Matt Haffigan? Do you remember me?

MATTHEW [*intentionally rude and blunt*] No. Who are you?

NORA. Oh, I'm sure you remember him, Mr Haffigan.

MATTHEW [*grudgingly admitting it*] I suppose he'll be young Larry Doyle that was.

LARRY. Yes

MATTHEW [*to Larry*] I hear you done well in America.

LARRY. Fairly well.

MATTHEW. I suppose you saw me brother Andy out dhere.

LARRY. No. It's such a big place that looking for a man there is like looking for a needle in a bundle of hay. They tell me he's a great man out there.

MATTHEW. So he is, God be praised. Wheres your father?

AUNT JUDY. He's inside, in the office, Mr Haffigan, with Barney Doarn n Father Dempsey.

Matthew, without wasting further words on the company, goes curtly into the house.

LARRY [*staring after him*] Is anything wrong with old Matt?

NORA. No. He's the same as ever. Why?

LARRY. He's not the same to me. He used to be very civil to Masther Larry: a deal too civil, I used to think. Now he's as surly and stand-off as a bear.

AUNT JUDY. Oh sure he's bought his farm in the Land Purchase. He's independent now.

NORA. It's made a great change, Larry. Youd harly know the old tenants now. Youd think it was a liberty to speak t'dhem – some o dhem. [*She goes to the table, and helps to take off the cloth, which she and Aunt Judy fold up between them*].

AUNT JUDY. I wonder what he wants to see Corny for. He hasnt been here since he paid the last of his old rent; and then he as good as threw it in Corny's face, I thought.

LARRY. No wonder! Of course they all hated us like the devil. Ugh! [*Moodily*] Ive seen them in that office, telling my father what a fine boy I was, and plastering him with compliments, with your honor here and your honor there, when all the time their fingers were itching to be at his throat.

AUNT JUDY. Deedn why should they want to hurt poor Corny? It was he that got Matt the lease of his farm, and stood up for him as an industrious decent man.

BROADBENT. Was he industrious? Thats remarkable, you know, in an Irishman.

LARRY. Industrious! That man's industry used to make me sick, even as a boy. I tell you, an Irish peasant's industry is not human: it's worse than the industry of a coral insect. An Englishman has some sense about working: he never does more than he can help – and hard enough to get him to do that without scamping it; but an Irishman will work as if he'd die the moment he stopped. That man Matthew Haffigan and his brother Andy made a farm out of a patch of stones on the hillside: cleared it and dug it with their own naked hands and bought their first spade out of their first crop of potatoes. Talk of making two blades of wheat grow where one grew before! those two men made a whole field of wheat grow where not even a furze bush had ever got its head up between the stones.

BROADBENT. That was magnificent, you know. Only a great race is capable of producing such men.

LARRY. Such fools, you mean! What good was it to them? The moment theyd done it, the landlord put a rent of £5 a year on them, and turned them out because they couldnt pay it.

AUNT JUDY. Why couldnt they pay as well as Billy Byrne that took it after them?

LARRY [*angrily*] You know very well that Billy Byrne never paid it. He only offered it to get possession. He never paid it.

AUNT JUDY. That was because Andy Haffigan hurt him with a brick so that he was never the same again. Andy had to run away to America for it.

BROADBENT [*glowing with indignation*] Who can blame him, Miss Doyle? Who can blame him?

LARRY [*impatiently*] Oh, rubbish! whats the good of the man thats starved out of a farm murdering the man thats starved into it? Would you have done such a thing?

BROADBENT. Yes. I – I – I – I – [*stammering with fury*] I should have shot the confounded landlord, and wrung the neck of the damned agent, and blown the farm up with dynamite, and Dublin Castle along with it.

LARRY. Oh yes: youd have done great things; and a fat lot of good youd have got out of it, too! Thats an Englishman all over! make bad laws and give away all the land, and then, when your economic incompetence produces its natural and inevitable results, get virtuously indignant and kill the people that carry out your laws.

AUNT JUDY. Sure never mind him, Mr Broadbent. It doesnt matter, anyhow, because theres harly any landlords left; and therll soon be none at all.

LARRY. On the contrary, therll soon be nothing else; and the Lord help Ireland then!

AUNT JUDY. Ah, youre never satisfied, Larry. [*To Nora*] Come on, alanna, an make the paste for the pie. We can leave them to their talk. They dont want us [*she takes up the tray and goes into the house*].

BROADBENT [*rising and gallantly protesting*] Oh, Miss Doyle! Really, really –

Nora, following Aunt Judy with the rolled-up cloth in her hands, looks at him and strikes him dumb. He watches her until she disappears; then comes to Larry and addresses him with sudden intensity.

BROADBENT. Larry.

LARRY. What is it?

BROADBENT. I got drunk last night, and proposed to Miss Reilly.

LARRY. You hwat??? [*He screams with laughter in the falsetto Irish register unused for that purpose in England*].

BROADBENT. What are you laughing at?

LARRY [*stopping dead*] I dont know. Thats the sort of thing an Irishman laughs at. Has she accepted you?

BROADBENT. I shall never forget that with the chivalry of her nation, though I was utterly at her mercy, she refused me.

LARRY. That was extremely improvident of her. [*Beginning to reflect*] But look here: when were you drunk? You were sober enough when you came back from the Round Tower with her.

BROADBENT. No, Larry, I was drunk, I am sorry to say. I had two tumblers of punch. She had to lead me home. You must have noticed it.

LARRY. I did not.

BROADBENT. She did.

LARRY. May I ask how long it took you to come to business? You can hardly have known her for more than a couple of hours.

BROADBENT. I am afraid it was hardly a couple of minutes. She was not here when I arrived; and I saw her for the first time at the tower.

LARRY. Well, you are a nice infant to be let loose in this country! Fancy the potcheen going to your head like that!

BROADBENT. Not to my head, I think. I have no headache; and I could speak distinctly. No: potcheen goes to the heart, not to the head. What ought I to do?

LARRY. Nothing. What need you do?

BROADBENT. There is rather a delicate moral question involved. The point is, was I drunk enough not to be morally responsible for my proposal? Or was I sober enough to be bound to repeat it now that I am undoubtedly sober?

LARRY. I should see a little more of her before deciding.

BROADBENT. No, no. That would not be right. That would not be fair. I am either under a moral obligation or I am not. I wish I knew how drunk I was.

LARRY. Well, you were evidently in a state of blithering sentimentality, anyhow.

BROADBENT. That is true, Larry: I admit it. Her voice has a most extraordinary effect on me. That Irish voice!

LARRY [sympathetically] Yes, I know. When I first went to London I very nearly proposed to walk out with a waitress in an Aerated Bread shop because her Whitechapel accent was so distinguished, so quaintly touching, so pretty —

BROADBENT [angrily] Miss Reilly is not a waitress, is she?

LARRY. Oh, come! The waitress was a very nice girl.

BROADBENT. You think every Englishwoman an angel. You really have coarse tastes in that way, Larry. Miss Reilly is one of the finer types: a type rare in England, except perhaps in the best of the aristocracy.

LARRY. Aristocracy be blowed! Do you know what Nora eats?

BROADBENT. Eats! what do you mean?

LARRY. Breakfast: tea and bread-and-butter, with an occasional rasher, and an egg on special occasions: say on her birthday. Dinner in the middle of the day, one course and nothing else. In the evening, tea and bread-and-butter again. You compare her with your English-women who wolf down from three to five meat meals a day; and naturally you find her a sylph. The difference is not a difference of type: it's the difference between the woman who eats not wisely but too well, and the woman who eats not wisely but too little.

BROADBENT [*furious*] Larry: you – you – you disgust me. You are a damned fool. [*He sits down angrily on the rustic seat, which sustains the shock with difficulty*].

LARRY. Steady! stead-eee! [*He laughs and seats himself on the table*].

Cornelius Doyle, Father Dempsey, Barney Doran, and Matthew Haffigan come from the house. Doran is a stout bodied, short armed, roundheaded, red haired man on the verge of middle age, of sanguine temperament, with an enormous capacity for derisive, obscene, blasphemous, or merely cruel and senseless fun, and a violent and impetuous intolerance of other temperaments and other opinions, all this representing energy and capacity wasted and demoralized by want of sufficient training and social pressure to force it into beneficent activity and build a character with it; for Barney is by no means either stupid or weak. He is recklessly untidy as to his person; but the worst effects of his neglect are mitigated by a powdering of flour and mill dust; and his unbrushed clothes, made of a fashionable tailor's sack-cloth, were evidently chosen regardless of expense for the sake of their appearance.

Matthew Haffigan, ill at ease, coasts the garden shyly on the shrubbery side until he anchors near the basket, where he feels least in the way. The priest comes to the table and slaps Larry on the shoulder. Larry, turning quickly, and recognizing Father Dempsey, alights from the table and shakes the priest's hand warmly. Doran comes down the garden between Father Dempsey and Matt; and Cornelius, on the other side of the table, turns to Broadbent, who rises genially.

CORNELIUS. I think we all met last night.

DORAN. I hadnt that pleasure.

CORNELIUS. To be sure, Barney: I forgot. [*To Broadbent, introducing Barney*] Mr Doran. He owns that fine mill you noticed from the car.

BROADBENT [*delighted with them all*] Most happy, Mr Doran. Very pleased indeed.

Doran, not quite sure whether he is being courted or patronized, nods independently.

DORAN. Hows yourself, Larry?

LARRY. Finely, thank you. No need to ask you [*Doran grins; and they shake hands*].

CORNELIUS. Give Father Dempsey a chair, Larry.

Matthew Haffigan runs to the nearest end of the table and takes the chair from it, placing it near the basket; but Larry has already taken the chair from the other end and placed it in front of the table. Father Dempsey accepts that more central position.

CORNELIUS. Sit down, Barney, will you; and you, Matt.

Doran takes the chair Matt is still offering to the priest; and poor Matthew, outfaced by the miller, humbly turns the basket upside down and sits on it. Cornelius brings his own breakfast chair from the table and sits down on Father Dempsey's right. Broadbent resumes his seat on the rustic bench. Larry crosses to the bench and is about to sit down beside him when Broadbent holds him off nervously.

BROADBENT. Do you think it will bear two, Larry?

LARRY. Perhaps not. Dont move. I'll stand. [*He posts himself behind the bench*].

They are all now seated, except Larry; and the session assumes a portentous air, as if something important were coming.

CORNELIUS. Praps youll explain, Father Dempsey.

FATHER DEMPSEY. No, no: go on, you: the Church has no politics.

CORNELIUS. Were yever thinkin o goin into parliament at all, Larry?

LARRY. Me!

FATHER DEMPSEY [*encouragingly*] Yes, you. Hwy not?

LARRY. I'm afraid my ideas would not be popular enough.

CORNELIUS. I dont know that. Do you, Barney?

DORAN. Theres too much blatherumskite in Irish politics: a dale too much.

LARRY. But what about your present member? Is he going to retire?

CORNELIUS. No: I dont know that he is.

LARRY [*interrogatively*] Well? then?

MATTHEW [*breaking out with surly bitterness*] Weve had enough of his foolish talk agen landlords. Hwat call has he to talk about the lan, that never was outside of a city office in his life?

CORNELIUS. We're tired of him. He doesnt know hwere to stop. Every man cant own land; and some men must own it to employ them. It was all very well when solid men like Doran an Matt were kep from ownin land. But hwat man in his senses ever wanted to give land to Patsy Farrll an dhe like o him?

BROADBENT. But surely Irish landlordism was accountable for what Mr Haffigan suffered.

MATTHEW. Never mind hwat I suffered. I know what I suffered adhout you tellin me. But did I ever ask for more dhan the farm I made wid me own hans? tell me that, Corny Doyle, and you that knows. Was I fit for the responsibility or was I not? [*Snarling angrily at Cornelius*] Am I to be compared to Patsy Farrll, that doesnt harly know his right hand from his left? What did he ever suffer, I'd like to know?

CORNELIUS. Thats just what I say. I wasnt comparin you to your disadvantage.

MATTHEW [*implacable*] Then hwat did you mane be talking about giving him lan?

DORAN. Aisy, Matt, aisy. Youre like a bear with a sore back.

MATTHEW [*trembling with rage*] An who are you, to offer to taitch me manners?

FATHER DEMPSEY [*admonitorily*] Now, now, now, Matt! none o dhat. How often have I told you youre too ready to take offence where none is meant? You dont understand: Corny Doyle is saying just what you want to have said. [*To Cornelius*] Go on, Mr Doyle; and never mind him.

MATTHEW [*rising*] Well, if me lan is to be given to Patsy and his like, I'm goin oura dhis. I –

DORAN [*with violent impatience*] Arra who's going to give your lan to Patsy, yowl fool ye?

FATHER DEMPSEY. Aisy, Barney, aisy. [*Sternly, to Matt*] I told you, Matthew Haffigan, that Corny Doyle was sayin nothin against you. I'm sorry your priest's word is not good enough for you. I'll go, sooner than stay to make you commit a sin against the Church. Good morning, gentlemen. [*He rises. They all rise, except Broadbent*].

DORAN [*to Matt*] There! Sarve you dam well right, you cantankerous oul noodle.

MATTHEW [*appalled*] Dont say dhat, Fadher Dempsey. I never had a thought agen you or the Holy Church. I know I'm a bit hasty when I think about the lan. I axe your pardon for it.

FATHER DEMPSEY [*resuming his seat with dignified reserve*] Very well: I'll overlook it this time. [*He sits down. The others sit down, except Matthew. Father Dempsey, about to ask Corny to proceed, remembers Matthew and turns to him, giving him just a crumb of graciousness*]. Sit down, Matt [*Matthew, crushed, sits down in disgrace, and is silent, his eyes shifting piteously from one speaker to another in an intensely mistrustful effort to understand them*]. Go on, Mr Doyle. We can make allowances. Go on.

CORNELIUS. Well, you see how it is, Larry. Round about here, weve got the land at last; and we want no more Government meddlin. We want a new class o man in parliament: one dhat knows dhat the farmer's the real backbone o the country, n doesnt care a snap of his fingers for the shoutn o the riff-raff in the towns, or for the foolishness of the laborers.

DORAN. Aye; and dhat can afford to live in London and pay his own way until Home Rule comes, instead of wantin subscriptions and the like.

FATHER DEMPSEY. Yes: thats a good point, Barney. When too much money goes to politics, it's the Church that has to starve for it. A member of parliament ought to be a help to the Church instead of a burden on it.

LARRY. Heres a chance for you, Tom. What do you say?

BROADBENT [*deprecatory, but important and smiling*] Oh, I have no claim whatever to the seat. Besides, I'm a Saxon.

DORAN. A hwat?

BROADBENT. A Saxon. An Englishman.

DORAN. An Englishman. Bedad I never heard it called that before.

MATTHEW [*cunningly*] If I might make so bould, Fadher, I wuldnt say but an English Prodestn mightnt have a more indepindent mind about the lan, an be less afeerd to spake out about it dhan an Irish Catholic.

CORNELIUS. But sure Larry's as good as English: arnt you, Larry?

LARRY. You may put me out of your head, father, once for all.

CORNELIUS. Arra why?

LARRY. I have strong opinions which wouldnt suit you.

DORAN [*rallying him blatantly*] Is it still Larry the bould Fenian?

LARRY. No: the bold Fenian is now an older and possibly foolisher man.

CORNELIUS. Hwat does it matter to us hwat your opinions are? You know that your father's bought his place here, just the same as Matt's farm n Barney's mill. All we ask now is to be let alone. Youve nothin against that, have you?

LARRY. Certainly I have. I dont believe in letting anybody or anything alone.

CORNELIUS [*losing his temper*] Arra what d'ye mean, you young fool? Here Ive got you the offer of a good seat in parliament; n you think yourself mighty smart to stand there and talk foolishness to me. Will you take it or leave it?

LARRY. Very well: I'll take it with pleasure if youll give it to me.

CORNELIUS [*subsiding sulkily*] Well, why couldnt you say so at once? It's a good job youve made up your mind at last.

DORAN [*suspiciously*] Stop a bit: stop a bit.

MATTHEW [*writhing between his dissatisfaction and his fear of the priest*] It's not because he's your son that he's to get the sate. Fadher Dempsey: wouldnt you think well to ask him what he manes about the lan?

LARRY [*coming down on Matt promptly*] I'll tell you, Matt. I always thought it was a stupid, lazy, good-for-nothing sort of thing to leave the land in the hands of the old landlords without calling them to a strict account for the use they made of it, and the condition of the people on it. I could see for myself that they thought of nothing but what they could get out of it to spend in England; and that they mortgaged and mortgaged until hardly one of them owned his own property or could have afforded to keep it up decently if he'd wanted to. But I tell you plump and plain, Matt, that if anybody thinks things will be any better now that the land is handed over to a lot of little men like you, without calling you to account either, theyre mistaken.

MATTHEW [*sullenly*] What call have you to look down on me? I suppose you think youre everybody because your father was a landagent.

LARRY. What call have you to look down on Patsy Farrell? I suppose you think youre everybody because you own a few fields.

MATTHEW. Was Patsy Farrll ever ill used as I was ill used? tell me dhat.

LARRY. He will be, if ever he gets into your power as you were in the power of your old landlord. Do you think, because youre poor and ignorant and half-crazy with toiling and moiling morning noon and night, that youll be any less greedy and oppressive to them that have no land at all than old Nick Lestrange, who was an educated travelled gentleman that would not have been tempted as hard by a hundred pounds as youd be by five shillings? Nick was too high above Patsy Farrell to be jealous of him; but you, that are only one little step above him, would die sooner than let him come up that step; and well you know it.

MATTHEW [*black with rage, in a low growl*] Lemmy oura dhis. [*He tries to rise; but Doran catches his coat and drags him down again*] I'm goin, I say. [*Raising his voice*] Leggo me coat, Barney Doran.

DORAN. Sit down, yowl omadhaun, you. [*Whispering*] Dont you want to stay an vote agen him?

FATHER DEMPSEY [*holding up his finger*] Matt! [*Matt subsides*]. Now, now, now! come, come! Hwats all dhis about Patsy Farrll? Hwy need you fall out about him?

LARRY. Because it was by using Patsy's poverty to undersell England in the markets of the world that we drove England to ruin Ireland. And she'll ruin us again the moment we lift our heads from the dust if we trade in cheap labor; and serve us right too! If I get into parliament, I'll try to get an Act to prevent any of you from giving Patsy less than a pound a week [*they all start, hardly able to believe their ears*] or working him harder than youd work a horse that cost you fifty guineas.

DORAN. Hwat!!!

CORNELIUS [*aghast*] A pound a – God save us! the boy's mad.

Matthew, feeling that here is something quite beyond his powers, turns openmouthed to the priest, as if looking for nothing less than the summary excommunication of Larry.

LARRY. How is the man to marry and live a decent life on less?

FATHER DEMPSEY. Man alive, hwere have you been living all these years? and hwat have you been dreaming of? Why, some o dhese honest men here cant make that much out o the land for dhemselves, much less give it to a laborer.

LARRY [*now thoroughly roused*] Then let them make room for those who can. Is Ireland never to have a chance? First she was given to the rich; and now that they have gorged on her flesh, her bones are to be flung to the poor, that can do nothing but suck the marrow out of her. If we cant have men of honor own the land, lets have men of ability. If we cant have men with ability, let us at least have men with capital. Anybody's better than Matt, who has neither honor, nor ability, nor capital, nor anything but mere brute labor and greed in him, Heaven help him!

DORAN. Well, we're not all foostherin oul doddherers like Matt. [*Pleasantly, to the subject of his description*] Are we, Matt?

LARRY. For modern industrial purposes you might just as well be, Barney. Youre all children: the big world that I belong to has gone past you and left you. Anyhow, we Irishmen were never made to be farmers; and we'll never do any good at it. We're like the Jews: the Almighty gave us brains, and bid us farm them and leave the clay and the worms alone.

FATHER DEMPSEY [*with gentle irony*] Oh! is it Jews you want to make of us? I must catechize you a bit meself, I think. The next thing youll be proposing is to repeal the disestablishment of the so-called Irish Church.

LARRY. Yes: why not? [*Sensation*].

MATTHEW [*rancorously*] He's a turncoat.

LARRY. St Peter, the rock on which our Church was built, was crucified head downwards for being a turncoat.

FATHER DEMPSEY [*with a quiet authoritative dignity which checks Doran, who is on the point of breaking out*] Thats true. You hold your tongue as befits your ignorance, Matthew Haffigan; and trust your priest to deal with this young man. Now, Larry Doyle, whatever the blessed St Peter was crucified for, it was not for being a Prodestan. Are you one?

LARRY. No. I am a Catholic intelligent enough to see that the Protestants are never more dangerous to us than when they are free from all alliances with the State. The so-called Irish Church is stronger today than ever it was.

MATTHEW. Fadher Dempsey: will you tell him dhat me mother's ant was shot and kilt dead in the sthreet o Rosscullen be a soljer in the tithe war? [*Frantically*] He wants to put the tithes on us again. He –

LARRY [*interrupting him with overbearing contempt*] Put the tithes on you again! Did the tithes ever come off you? Was your land any dearer when you paid the tithe to the parson than it was when you paid the same money to Nick Lestrange as rent, and he handed it over to the Church Sustentation Fund? Will you always be duped by Acts of Parliament that change nothing but the necktie of the man that picks your pocket? I'll tell you what I'd do with you, Matt Haffigan; I'd make you pay tithes to your own Church. I want the Catholic Church established in Ireland: thats what I want. Do you think that I, brought up to regard myself as the son of a great and holy Church, can bear to see her begging her bread from the ignorance and superstition of men like you? I would have her as high above worldly want as I would have her above worldly pride or ambition. Aye; and I woul¹ have Ireland compete with Rome itself for the chair of St Peter and the citadel of the Church; for Rome, in spite of all the blood of the martyrs, is pagan at heart to this day, while in Ireland the people is the Church and the Church the people.

FATHER DEMPSEY [*startled but not at all displeased*] Whisht, man! youre worse than mad Pether Keegan himself.

BROADBENT [*who has listened in the greatest astonishment*] You amaze me, Larry. Who would have thought of your coming out like this! [*Solemnly*] But much as I appreciate your really brilliant eloquence, I implore you not to desert the great Liberal principle of Disestablishment.

LARRY. I am not a Liberal: Heaven forbid! A disestablished Church is the worst tyranny a nation can groan under.

BROADBENT [*making a wry face*] Dont be paradoxical, Larry. It really gives me a pain in my stomach.

LARRY. Youll soon find out the truth of it here. Look at Father Dempsey! he is disestablished: he has nothing to hope or fear from the State; and the result is that he's the most powerful man in Rosscullen. The member for Rosscullen would shake in his shoes if Father Dempsey looked crooked at him. [*Father Dempsey smiles, by no means averse to this acknowledgment of his authority*]. Look at yourself! you would defy the established Archbishop of Canterbury ten times a day; but catch you daring to say a word that would shock a Nonconformist! not you. The Conservative party today is the only one thats not priest-ridden – excuse the expression, Father [*Father Dempsey nods tolerantly*]

– because it's the only one that has established its Church and can prevent a clergyman becoming a bishop if he's not a Statesman as well as a Churchman.

He stops. They stare at him dumbfounded, and leave it to the priest to answer him.

FATHER DEMPSEY [*judicially*] Young man: youll not be the member for Rosscullen; but dheres more in your head than the comb will take out.

LARRY. I'm sorry to disappoint you, Father; but I told you it would be no use. And now I think the candidate had better retire and leave you to discuss his successor. [*He takes a newspaper from the table and goes away through the shrubbery amid dead silence, all turning to watch him until he passes out of sight round the corner of the house*].

DORAN [*dazed*] Hwat sort of a fella is he at all at all?

FATHER DEMPSEY. He's a clever lad: dheres the making of a man in him yet.

MATTHEW [*in consternation*] D'ye mane to say dhat yll put him into parliament to bring back Nick Lesthrange on me, and to put tithes on me, and to rob me for the like o Patsy Farrll, because he's Corny Doyle's son?

DORAN [*brutally*] Arra hould your whisht: who's going to send him into parliament? Maybe youd like us to send you dhere to thrate dhem to a little o your anxiety about dhat dirty little podato patch o yours.

MATTHEW [*plaintively*] Am I to be towld dhis afther all me sufferins?

DORAN. Och, I'm tired o your sufferins. Weve been hearin nothin else ever since we was childher but sufferins. Hwen it wasnt yours it was somebody else's; and hwen it was nobody else's it was ould Irelan's. How the divil are we to live on wan anodher's sufferins?

FATHER DEMPSEY. Thats a thrue word, Barney Doran; only your tongue's a little too familiar wi dhe divil. [*To Matt*] If youd think a little more o the sufferins of the blessed saints, Matt, an a little less o your own, youd find the way shorter from your farm to heaven [*Matt is about to reply*] Dhere now! dhats enough! we know you mean well; an I'm not angry with you.

BROADBENT. Surely, Mr Haffigan, you can see the simple explanation of all this. My friend Larry Doyle is a most brilliant speaker; but he's a Tory: an ingrained old-fashioned Tory.

CORNELIUS. N how d'ye make dhat out, if I might ask you, Mr Broadbent?

BROADBENT [*collecting himself for a political deliverance*] Well, you know, Mr Doyle, theres a strong dash of Toryism in the Irish character. Larry himself says that the great Duke of Wellington was the most typical Irishman that ever lived. Of course thats an absurd paradox; but still theres a great deal of truth in it. Now I am a Liberal. You know the great principles of the Liberal Party. Peace –

FATHER DEMPSEY [*piously*] Hear! hear!

BROADBENT [*encouraged*] Thank you. Retrenchment – [*he waits for further applause*].

MATTHEW [*timidly*] What might rethrenchment mane now?

BROADBENT. It means an immense reduction in the burden of the rates and taxes.

MATTHEW [*respectfully approving*] Dhats right. Dhats right, sir.

BROADBENT [*perfunctorily*] And, of course, Reform.

CORNELIUS
FATHER DEMPSEY } [*conventionally*] Of course.
DORAN

MATTHEW [*still suspicious*] Hwat does Reform mane, sir? Does it mane altherin annythin dhats as it is now?

BROADBENT [*impressively*] It means, Mr Haffigan, maintaining those reforms which have already been conferred on humanity by the Liberal Party, and trusting for future developments to the free activity of a free people on the basis of those reforms.

DORAN. Dhats right. No more meddlin. We're all right now: all we want is to be let alone.

CORNELIUS. Hwat about Home Rule?

BROADBENT [*rising so as to address them more imposingly*] I really cannot tell you what I feel about Home Rule without using the language of hyperbole.

DORAN. Savin Fadher Dempsey's presence, eh?

BROADBENT [*not understanding him*] Quite so – er – oh yes. All I can say is that as an Englishman I blush for the Union. It is the blackest stain on our national history. I look forward to the time – and it cannot be far distant, gentlemen, because Humanity is looking forward to it too, and insisting on it with no uncertain voice – I look forward to the time when an Irish legislature shall arise once more on the emerald pasture of College Green, and the Union Jack – that detestable symbol of a decadent Imperialism – be replaced by a flag as green as the island over which it waves: a flag on which we shall ask for England only a modest quartering in memory of our great party and of the immortal name of our grand old leader.

DORAN [*enthusiastically*] Dhats the style, begob! [*He smites his knee, and winks at Matt*].

MATTHEW. More power to you, sir!

BROADBENT. I shall leave you now, gentlemen, to your deliberations. I should like to have enlarged on the services rendered by the Liberal Party to the religious faith of the great majority of the people of Ireland; but I shall content myself with saying that in my opinion you should choose no representative who – no matter what his personal creed may be – is not an ardent supporter of freedom of conscience, and is not prepared to prove it by contributions, as lavish as his means will allow, to the great and beneficent work which you, Father Dempsey [*Father Dempsey bows*], are doing for the people of Rosscullen. Nor should the lighter, but still most important question of the sports of the people be forgotten. The local cricket club –

CORNELIUS. The hwat!

DORAN. Nobody plays bat n ball here, if dhats what you mane.

BROADBENT. Well, let us say quoits. I saw two men, I think, last night – but after all, these are questions of detail. The main thing is that your candidate, whoever he may be, shall be a man of some means, able to help the locality instead of burdening it. And if he were a countryman of my own, the moral effect on the House of Commons would be immense! tremendous! Pardon my saying these few words: nobody feels their impertinence more than I do. Good morning, gentlemen.

He turns impressively to the gate, and trots away, congratulating himself, with a little twist of his head and cock of his eye, on having done a good stroke of political business.

MATTHEW [*awestruck*] Good morning, sir.

THE REST. Good morning. [*They watch him vacantly until he is out of earshot*].

CORNELIUS. Hwat d'ye think, Father Dempsey?

FATHER DEMPSEY [*indulgently*] Well, he hasnt much sense, God help him; but for the matter o that, neether has our present member.

DORAN. Arra musha he's good enough for parliament: what is there to do there but gas a bit, an chivy the Government, an vote wi dh Irish party?

CORNELIUS [*ruminatively*] He's the queerest Englishman *I* ever met. When he opened the paper dhis mornin the first thing he saw was that an English expedition had been bet in a battle in Inja somewhere; an he was as pleased as Punch! Larry told him that if he'd been alive when the news o Waterloo came, he'd a died o grief over it. Bedad I dont think he's quite right in his head.

DORAN. Divil a matther if he has plenty o money. He'll do for us right enough.

MATTHEW [*deeply impressed by Broadbent, and unable to understand their levity concerning him*] Did you mind what he said about rethrenchment? That was very good, I thought.

FATHER DEMPSEY. You might find out from Larry, Corny, what his means are. God forgive us all! it's poor work spoiling the Egyptians, though we have good warrant for it; so I'd like to know how much spoil there is before I commit meself. [*He rises. They all rise respectfully*].

CORNELIUS [*ruefully*] I'd set me mind on Larry himself for the seat; but I suppose it cant be helped.

FATHER DEMPSEY [*consoling him*] Well, the boy's young yet; an he has a head on him. Goodbye, all. [*He goes out through the gate*].

DORAN. I must be goin, too. [*He directs Cornelius's attention to what is passing in the road*]. Look at me bould Englishman shakin hans wid Fadher Dempsey for all the world like a candidate on election day. And look at Fadher Dempsey givin him a squeeze an a wink as much as to say It's all right, me boy. You watch him shakin hans with me too: he's waitn for me. I'll tell him he's as good as elected. [*He goes, chuckling mischievously*].

CORNELIUS. Come in with me, Matt. I think I'll sell you the pig after all. Come in an wet the bargain.

MATTHEW [*instantly dropping into the old whine of the tenant*] I'm afeerd I cant afford the price, sir. [*He follows Cornelius into the house*].

Larry, newspaper still in hand, comes back through the shrubbery. Broadbent returns through the gate.

LARRY. Well? What has happened?

BROADBENT [*hugely self-satisfied*] I think Ive done the trick this time. I just gave them a bit of straight talk; and it went home. They were greatly impressed: everyone of those men believes in me and will vote for me when the question of selecting a candidate comes up. After all, whatever you say, Larry, they like an Englishman. They feel they can trust him, I suppose.

LARRY. Oh! theyve transferred the honor to you, have they?

BROADBENT [*complacently*] Well, it was a pretty obvious move, I should think. You know, these fellows have plenty of shrewdness in spite of their Irish oddity. [*Hodson comes from the house. Larry sits in Doran's chair and reads*]. Oh, by the way, Hodson –

HODSON [*coming between Broadbent and Larry*] Yes, sir?

BROADBENT. I want you to be rather particular as to how you treat the people here.

HODSON. I havnt treated any of em yet, sir. If I was to accept all the treats they offer me I shouldnt be able to stand at this present moment, sir.

BROADBENT. Oh well, dont be too stand-offish, you know, Hodson. I should like you to be popular. If it costs anything I'll make it up to you. It doesnt matter if you get a bit upset at first: theyll like you all the better for it.

HODSON. I'm sure youre very kind, sir; but it dont seem to matter to me whether they like me or not. I'm not going to stand for parliament here, sir.

BROADBENT. Well, I am. Now do you understand?

HODSON [*waking up at once*] Oh, I beg your pardon, sir, I'm sure. I understand, sir.

CORNELIUS [*appearing at the house door with Matt*] Patsy'll drive the pig over this evenin, Matt. Goodbye. [*He goes back into the house. Matt makes for the gate. Broadbent stops him. Hodson, pained by the derelict basket, picks it up and carries it away behind the house*].

BROADBENT [*beaming candidatorially*] I must thank you very particularly, Mr Haffigan, for your support this morning. I value it because I know that the real heart of a nation is the class you represent, the yeomanry.

MATTHEW [*aghast*] The yeomanry!!!

LARRY [*looking up from his paper*] Take care, Tom! In Rosscullen a yeoman means a sort of Orange Bashi-Bazouk. In England, Matt, they call a freehold farmer a yeoman.

MATTHEW [*huffily*] I dont need to be insthructed be you, Larry Doyle. Some people think no one knows anythin but dhemselves. [*To Broadbent, deferentially*] Of course I know a gentleman like you would not compare me to the yeomanry. Me own granfather was flogged in the sthreets of Athenmullet be them when they put a gun in the thatch of his house and then went and found it there, bad cess to them!

BROADBENT [*with sympathetic interest*] Then you are not the first martyr of your family, Mr Haffigan?

MATTHEW. They turned me out o the farm I made out of the stones o Little Rosscullen hill wid me own hans.

BROADBENT. I have heard about it; and my blood still boils at the thought. [*Calling*] Hodson –

HODSON [*behind the corner of the house*] Yes, sir. [*He hurries forward*].

BROADBENT. Hodson: this gentleman's sufferings should make every Englishman think. It is want of thought rather than want of heart that allows such iniquities to disgrace society.

HODSON [*prosaically*] Yes, sir.

MATTHEW. Well, I'll be goin. Good mornin to you kindly, sir.

BROADBENT. You have some distance to go, Mr Haffigan: will you allow me to drive you home?

MATTHEW. Oh sure it'd be throublin your honor.

BROADBENT. I insist: it will give me the greatest pleasure, I assure you. My car is in the stable: I can get it round in five minutes.

MATTHEW. Well, sir, if you wouldnt mind, we could bring the pig Ive just bought from Corny –

BROADBENT [*with enthusiasm*] Certainly, Mr Haffigan: it will be quite delightful to drive with a pig in the car: I shall feel quite like an Irishman. Hodson: stay with Mr Haffigan; and give him a hand with the pig if necessary. Come, Larry; and help me. [*He rushes away through the shrubbery*].

LARRY [*throwing the paper ill-humoredly on the chair*] Look here, Tom! here, I say! confound it! – [*he runs after him*].

MATTHEW [*glowering disdainfully at Hodson, and sitting down on Cornelius's chair as an act of social self-assertion*] N are you the valley?

HODSON. The valley? Oh, I follow you: yes: I'm Mr Broadbent's valet.

MATTHEW. Ye have an aisy time of it: you look purty sleek. [*With suppressed ferocity*] Look at me! Do *I* look sleek?

HODSON [*sadly*] I wish I ad your ealth: you look as ard as nails. I suffer from an excess of uric acid.

MATTHEW. Musha what sort o disease is zhourag-assid? Didjever suffer from injustice and starvation? Dhats the Irish disease. It's aisy for you to talk o sufferin, and you livin on the fat o the land wid money wrung from us.

HODSON [*suddenly dropping the well-spoken valet, and breaking out in his native cockney*] Wots wrong with you, aold chep? Ez ennybody been doin ennythink to you?

MATTHEW. Anythin timmy! Didnt your English masther say that the blood biled in him to hear the way they put a rint on me for the farm I made wid me own hans, an turned me out of it to give it to Billy Byrne?

HODSON. Ow, Tom Broadbent's blad boils pretty easy over ennything that eppens aht of his aown cantry. Downt you be tiken in by my aowl men, Peddy.

MATTHEW [*indignantly*] Paddy yourself! How dar you call me Paddy?

HODSON [*unmoved*] You jast keep your air on and listen to me. You Awrish people are too well off: thets wots the metter with you. [*With sudden passion*] You talk of your rotten little fawm cause you mide it by chackin a few stowns dahn a ill! Well, wot prawce maw grenfawther, Oi should lawk to knaow, that fitted ap a fust clawss shop and built ap a fust clawss dripery business in Landon by sixty years work, and then was chacked aht of it on is ed at the end of is lease withaht a penny for his goodwill. You talk of evictions! you that cawnt be moved until youve ran ap ighteen months rent. Oi once ran ap four weeks in Lembeth wen Oi was aht of a job in winter. They took the door off its inges and the winder aht of its seshes on me, and gev maw wawf pnoomownia. Oi'm a widower nah. [*Between his teeth*] Gawd! when Oi think of the things we Englishmen as to pat ap with, and eah you Awrish ahlin abaht your silly little grievances, and see the wy you mike it worse for haz by the rotten wiges youll cam over and tike and the rotten plices youll sleep in, I jast feel that I could tike the aowl bloomin British awland and mike you a present of it, jast to let you fawnd aht wot reel awdship's lawk.

MATTHEW [*starting up, more in scandalized incredulity than in anger*] D'ye have the face to set up England agen Ireland for injustices an wrongs an disthress an sufferin?

HODSON [*with intense disgust and contempt*] Ow, chack it, Paddy. Cheese it. You danno wot awdship is owver eah: all you knaow is ah to ahl abaht it. You tike the biscuit at thet, you do. Oi'm a Owm Ruler, Oi em. Do you knaow woy?

MATTHEW [*equally contemptuous*] D'ye know, yourself?

HODSON. Yus Oi do. It's because Oi want a little attention pide to my aown cantry; and thetll never be as long as your cheps are ollerin at Westminster as if nowbody mettered but your own bloomin selves. Send em back to ell or C'naught, as good aowld English Cramwell said. I'm jast sick of Awrland. Let it gow. Cat the caible. Mike it a present to Germany to keep the aowl Kyzer busy for a wawl; and give poor aowld England a chawnce: thets wot Oi sy.

MATTHEW [*full of scorn for a man so ignorant as to be unable to pronounce the word Connaught, which practically rhymes with bonnet in Ireland, though in Hodson's dialect it rhymes with untaught*] Take care we dont cut the cable ourselves some day, bad scran to you! An tell me dhis: have yanny Coercion Acs in England? Have yanny Removable magisthruts? Have you Dublin Castle to suppress every newspaper dhat takes the part o your own counthry?

HODSON. We can beyive ahrselves withaht sich things.

MATTHEW. Bedad youre right. It'd ony be waste o time to muzzle a sheep. Here! wheres me pig? God forgimmy for talkin to a poor ignorant craycher like you!

HODSON [*grinning with good-humored malice, too convinced of his own superiority to feel his withers wrung*] Your pig'll ev a rare doin in that car, Peddy. Forty mawl an ahr dahn that rocky line will strawk it pretty pink, you bet.

MATTHEW [*scornfully*] Hwy cant you tell a raisonable lie when youre about it? What horse can go forty mile an hour?

HODSON. Orse! Wy, you silly aowl rotter, it's not a orse: it's a mowtor. Do you spowse Tom Broadbent ud gow himself to fetch a orse?

MATTHEW [*in consternation*] Holy Moses! dont tell me it's the ingine he wants to take me on.

HODSON. Wot else?

MATTHEW. Your sowl to Morris Kelly! why didnt you tell me that before? The divil an ingine he'll get me on this day. [*His ear catches an approaching teuf–teuf*]. Oh murdher! it's comin afther me: I hear the puff-puff of it. [*He runs away through the gate, much to Hodson's amusement. The noise of the motor ceases; and Hodson, anticipating Broadbent's return, throws off the cockney and recomposes himself as a valet. Broadbent and Larry come through the shrubbery. Hodson moves aside to the gate*].

BROADBENT. Where is Mr Haffigan? Has he gone for the pig?

HODSON. Bolted, sir. Afraid of the motor, sir.

BROADBENT [*much disappointed*] Oh, thats very tiresome. Did he leave any message?

HODSON. He was in too great a hurry, sir. Started to run home, sir, and left his pig behind him.

BROADBENT [*eagerly*] Left the pig! Then it's all right. The pig's the thing: the pig will win over every Irish heart to me. We'll take the pig home to Haffigan's farm in the motor: it will have a tremendous effect. Hodson!

HODSON. Yes, sir?

BROADBENT. Do you think you could collect a crowd to see the motor?

HODSON. Well, I'll try, sir.

BROADBENT. Thank you, Hodson: do.

Hodson goes out through the gate.

LARRY [*desperately*] Once more, Tom, will you listen to me?

BROADBENT. Rubbish! I tell you it will be all right.

LARRY. Only this morning you confessed how surprised you were to find that the people here shewed no sense of humor.

BROADBENT [*suddenly very solemn*] Yes: their sense of humor is in abeyance: I noticed it the moment we landed. Think of that in a country where every man is a born humorist! Think of what it means! [*Impressively*] Larry: we are in the presence of a great national grief.

LARRY. Whats to grieve them?

BROADBENT. I divined it, Larry: I saw it in their faces. Ireland has never smiled since her hopes were buried in the grave of Gladstone.

LARRY. Oh, whats the use of talking to such a man? Now look here, Tom. Be serious for a moment if you can.

BROADBENT [*stupent*] Serious! I!!!

LARRY. Yes, you. You say the Irish sense of humor is in abeyance. Well, if you drive through Rosscullen in a motor car with Haffigan's pig, it wont stay in abeyance. Now I warn you.

BROADBENT [*breezily*] Why, so much the better! I shall enjoy the joke myself more than any of them. [*Shouting*] Hallo, Patsy Farrell, where are you?

PATSY [*appearing in the shrubbery*] Here I am, your honor.

BROADBENT. Go and catch the pig and put it into the car: we're going to take it to Mr Haffigan's. [*He gives Larry a slap on the shoulders that sends him staggering off through the gate, and follows him buoyantly, exclaiming*] Come on, you old croaker! I'll shew you how to win an Irish seat.

PATSY [*meditatively*] Bedad, if dhat pig gets a howlt o the handle o the machine – [*He shakes his head ominously and drifts away to the pigsty*].

ACT IV

The parlor in Cornelius Doyle's house. It communicates with the garden by a half glazed door. The fireplace is at the other side of the room, opposite the door and windows, the architect not having been sensitive to draughts. The table, rescued from the garden, is in the middle; and at it sits Keegan, the central figure in a rather crowded apartment. Nora, sitting with her back to the fire at the end of the table, is playing backgammon across its corner with him, on his left hand. Aunt Judy, a little further back, sits facing the fire knitting, with her feet on the fender. A little to Keegan's right, in front of the table, and almost sitting on it, is Barney Doran. Half a dozen friends of his, all men, are between him and the open door, supported by others outside. In the corner behind them is the sofa, of mahogany and horsehair, made up as a bed for Broadbent. Against the wall behind Keegan stands a mahogany sideboard. A door leading to the interior of the house is near the fireplace, behind Aunt Judy. There are chairs against the wall, one at each end of the sideboard. Keegan's hat is on the one nearest the inner door; and his stick is leaning against it. A third chair, also against the wall, is near the garden door.

There is a strong contrast of emotional atmosphere between the two sides of the room. Keegan is extraordinarily stern: no game of backgammon could possibly make a man's face so grim. Aunt Judy is quietly busy. Nora is trying to ignore Doran and attend to her game.

On the other hand Doran is reeling in an ecstasy of mischievous mirth which has infected all his friends. They are screaming with laughter, doubled up, leaning on the furniture and against the walls, shouting, screeching, crying.

AUNT JUDY [*as the noise lulls for a moment*] Arra hold your noise, Barney. What is there to laugh at?

DORAN. It got its fut into the little hweel – [*he is overcome afresh: and the rest collapse again*].

AUNT JUDY. Ah, have some sense: youre like a parcel o childher. Nora: hit him a thump on the back: he'll have a fit.

DORAN [*with squeezed eyes, exsufflicate with cachinnation*] Frens, he sez to dhem outside Doolan's: I'm takin the gintleman that pays the rint for a dhrive.

AUNT JUDY. Who did he mean be that?

DORAN. They call a pig that in England. Thats their notion of a joke.

AUNT JUDY. Musha God help them if they can joke no better than that!

DORAN [*with renewed symptoms*] Thin –

AUNT JUDY. Ah now dont be tellin it all over and settin yourself off again, Barney.

NORA. Youve told us three times, Mr Doran.

DORAN. Well but whin I think of it –!

AUNT JUDY. Then dont think of it, alanna.

DORAN. Dhere was Patsy Farrll in the back sate wi dhe pig between his knees, n me bould English boyoh in front at the machinery, n Larry Doyle in the road startin the injine wid a bed winch. At the first puff of it the pig lep out of its skin and bled Patsy's nose wi dhe ring in its snout. [*Roars of laughter: Keegan glares at them*]. Before Broadbint knew hwere he was, the pig was up his back and over into his lap; and bedad the poor baste did credit to Corny's thrainin of it; for it put in the fourth speed wid its right crubeen as if it was enthered for the Gordn Bennett.

NORA [*reproachfully*] And Larry in front of it and all! It's nothin to laugh at, Mr Doran.

DORAN. Bedad, Miss Reilly, Larry cleared six yards sideways at wan jump if he cleared an inch; and he'd a cleared seven if Doolan's granmother hadnt cotch him in her apern widhout intindin to. [*Immense merriment*].

AUNT JUDY. Ah, for shame, Barney! the poor old woman! An she was hurt before, too, when she slipped on the stairs.

DORAN. Bedad, maam, she's hurt behind now; for Larry bouled her over like a skittle. [*General delight at this typical stroke of Irish Rabelaisianism*].

NORA. It's well Mr Doyle wasnt killed.

DORAN. Faith it wasnt o Larry we were thinkin jus dhen, wi dhe pig takin the main sthreet o Rosscullen on market day at a mile a minnit. Dh ony thing Broadbint could get at wi dhe pig in front of him was a fut brake; n the pig's tail was undher dhat; so that whin he thought he was putn non the brake he was ony squeezin the life out o the pig's tail. The more he put the brake on the more the pig squealed n the fasther he dhruv.

AUNT JUDY. Why couldnt he throw the pig out into the road?

DORAN. Sure he couldnt stand up to it, because he was spanchelled-like between his seat and dhat thing like a wheel on top of a stick between his knees.

AUNT JUDY. Lord have mercy on us!

NORA. I dont know how you can laugh. Do you, Mr Keegan?

KEEGAN [grimly] Why not? There is danger, destruction, torment! What more do we need to make us merry? Go on, Barney: the last drops of joy are not squeezed from the story yet. Tell us again how our brother was torn asunder.

DORAN [puzzled] Whose bruddher?

KEEGAN. Mine.

NORA. He means the pig, Mr Doran. You know his way.

DORAN [rising gallantly to the occasion] Bedad I'm sorry for your poor bruddher, Misther Keegan; but I recommend you to thry him wid a couple o fried eggs for your breakfast tomorrow. It was a case of Excelsior wi dhat ambitious baste; for not content wid jumpin from the back seat into the front wan, he jumped from the front wan into the road in front of the car. And –

KEEGAN. And everybody laughed!

NORA. Dont go over that again, please, Mr Doran.

DORAN. Faith be the time the car went over the poor pig dhere was little left for me or anywan else to go over except wid a knife an fork.

AUNT JUDY. Why didnt Mr Broadbent stop the car when the pig was gone?

DORAN. Stop the car! He might as well ha tried to stop a mad bull. First it went wan way an made fireworks o Molly Ryan's crockery stall; an dhen it slewed round an ripped ten fut o wall out o the corner o the pound. [With enormous enjoyment] Begob, it just tore the town in two and sent the whole dam market to blazes. [Nora offended, rises].

KEEGAN [indignantly] Sir!

DORAN [quickly] Savin your presence, Miss Reilly, and Misther Keegan's. Dhere! I wont say anuddher word.

NORA. I'm surprised at you, Mr Doran. [She sits down again].

DORAN [reflectively] He has the divil's own luck, that Englishman, annyway; for hwen they picked him up he hadnt a scratch on him, barrn hwat the pig did to his cloes. Patsy had two fingers out o jynt; but the smith pulled them sthraight for him. Oh, you never heard such a hullaballoo as there was. There was Molly cryin Me chaney, me beautyful chaney! n oul Matt shoutin Me pig, me pig! n the polus takin the number o the car, n not a man in the town able to speak for laughin —

KEEGAN [with intense emphasis] It is hell: it is hell. Nowhere else could such a scene be a burst of happiness for the people.

Cornelius comes in hastily from the garden, pushing his way through the little crowd.

CORNELIUS. Whisht your laughin, boys! Here he is. [*He puts his hat on the sideboard, and goes to the fireplace, where he posts himself with his back to the chimneypiece*].

AUNT JUDY. Remember your behavior now.

Everybody becomes silent, solemn, concerned, sympathetic. Broadbent enters, soiled and disordered as to his motoring coat: immensely important and serious as to himself. He makes his way to the end of the table nearest the garden door, whilst Larry, who accompanies him, throws his motoring coat on the sofa bed, and sits down, watching the proceedings.

BROADBENT [*taking off his leather cap with dignity and placing it on the table*] I hope you have not been anxious about me.

AUNT JUDY. Deedn we have, Mr Broadbent. It's a mercy you werent killed.

DORAN. Kilt! It's a mercy dheres two bones of you left houldin together. How dijjescape at all at all? Well, I never thought I'd be so glad to see you safe and sound again. Not a man in the town would say less [*murmurs of kindly assent*]. Wont you come down to Doolan's and have a dhrop o brandy to take the shock off?

BROADBENT. Youre all really too kind; but the shock has quite passed off.

DORAN [*jovially*] Never mind. Come along all the same and tell us about it over a frenly glass.

BROADBENT. May I say how deeply I feel the kindness with which I have been overwhelmed since my accident? I can truthfully declare that I am glad it happened, because it has brought out the kindness and sympathy of the Irish character to an extent I had no conception of.

SEVERAL
PRESENT
{ Oh, sure youre welcome!
Sure it's only natural.
Sure you might have been kilt.

A young man, feeling that he must laugh or burst, hurries out. Barney puts an iron constraint on his features.

BROADBENT. All I can say is that I wish I could drink the health of everyone of you.

DORAN. Dhen come an do it.

BROADBENT [*very solemnly*] No: I am a teetotaller.

AUNT JUDY [*incredulously*] Arra since when?

BROADBENT. Since this morning, Miss Doyle. I have had a lesson [*he looks at Nora significantly*] that I shall not forget. It may be that total abstinence has already saved my life; for I was astonished at the steadiness of my nerves when death stared me in the face today. So I will ask you to excuse me. [*He collects himself for a speech*]. Gentlemen: I hope the gravity of the peril through which we have all passed – for I know that the danger to the bystanders was as great as to the occupants of the car – will prove an earnest of closer and more serious relations between us in the future. We have had a somewhat agitating day: a valuable and innocent animal has lost its life: a public building has been wrecked: an aged and infirm lady has suffered an impact for which I feel personally responsible, though my old friend Mr Laurence Doyle unfortunately incurred the first effects of her very natural resentment. I greatly regret the damage to Mr Patrick Farrell's fingers; and I have of course taken care that he shall not suffer pecuniarily by his mishap. [*Murmurs of admiration at his magnanimity, and A Voice* 'Youre a gentleman, sir']. I am glad to say that Patsy took it like an Irishman, and, far from expressing any vindictive feeling, declared his willingness to break all his fingers and toes for me on the same terms [*subdued applause, and* 'More power to Patsy!']. Gentlemen: I felt at home in Ireland from the first [*rising excitement among his hearers*]. In every Irish breast I have found that spirit of liberty [*A cheery voice* 'Hear hear'], that instinctive mistrust of the Government [*A small pious voice, with intense expression,* 'God bless you, sir!'], that love of independence [*A defiant voice,* 'Thats it! Independence!'], that indignant sympathy with the cause of oppressed nationalities abroad [*A threatening growl from all: the ground-swell of patriotic passion*] and with the resolute assertion of personal rights at home, which is all but extinct in my own country. If it were legally possible I should become a naturalized Irishman; and if ever it be my good fortune to represent an Irish constituency in parliament, it shall be my first care to introduce a Bill legalizing such an operation. I believe a large section of the Liberal party would avail themselves of it. [*Momentary scepticism*] I do. [*Convulsive cheering*]. Gentlemen: I have said enough. [*Cries of* 'Go on']. No: I have as yet no right to address you at all on political subjects; and we must not abuse the warm-hearted Irish hospitality of Miss Doyle by turning her sitting room into a public meeting.

DORAN [*energetically*] Three cheers for Tom Broadbent, the future member for Rosscullen!

AUNT JUDY [*waving a half knitted sock*] Hip hip hurray!

The cheers are given with great heartiness, as it is by this time, for the more humorous spirits present, a question of vociferation or internal rupture.

BROADBENT. Thank you from the bottom of my heart, friends.

NORA [*whispering to Doran*] Take them away, Mr Doran [*Doran nods*].

DORAN. Well, good evenin, Mr Broadbent; an may you never regret the day you wint dhrivin wid Haffigan's pig! [*They shake hands*]. Good evenin, Miss Doyle.

General handshaking, Broadbent shaking hands with everybody effusively. He accompanies them to the garden and can be heard outside saying Good night in every inflexion known to parliamentary candidates. Nora, Aunt Judy, Keegan, Larry, and Cornelius are left in the parlor. Larry goes to the threshold and watches the scene in the garden.

NORA. It's a shame to make game of him like that. He's a gradle more good in him than Barney Doran.

CORNELIUS. It's all up with his candidature. He'll be laughed out o the town.

LARRY [*turning quickly from the doorway*] Oh no he wont: he's not an Irishman. He'll never know theyre laughing at him; and while theyre laughing he'll win the seat.

CORNELIUS. But he cant prevent the story getting about.

LARRY. He wont want to. He'll tell it himself as one of the most providential episodes in the history of England and Ireland.

AUNT JUDY. Sure he wouldnt make a fool of himself like that.

LARRY. Are you sure he's such a fool after all, Aunt Judy? Suppose you had a vote! which would you rather give it to? the man that told the story of Haffigan's pig Barney Doran's way or Broadbent's way?

AUNT JUDY. Faith I wouldnt give it to a man at all. It's a few women they want in parliament to stop their foolish blather.

BROADBENT [*bustling into the room, and taking off his damaged motoring overcoat, which he puts down on the sofa*] Well thats over. I must apologize for making a speech, Miss Doyle; but they like it, you know. Everything helps in electioneering.

Larry takes the chair near the door; draws it near the table; and sits astride it, with his elbows folded on the back.

AUNT JUDY. I'd no notion you were such an orator, Mr Broadbent.

BROADBENT. Oh, it's only a knack. One picks it up on the platform. It stokes up their enthusiasm.

AUNT JUDY. Oh, I forgot. Youve not met Mr Keegan. Let me introjoosha.

BROADBENT [*shaking hands effusively*] Most happy to meet you, Mr Keegan. I have heard of you, though I have not had the pleasure of shaking your hand before. And now may I ask you – for I value no man's opinion more – what you think of my chances here.

KEEGAN [*coldly*] Your chances, sir, are excellent. You will get into parliament.

BROADBENT [*delighted*] I hope so. I think so. [*Fluctuating*] You really think so? You are sure you are not allowing your enthusiasm for our principles to get the better of your judgment?

KEEGAN. I have no enthusiasm for your principles, sir. You will get into parliament because you want to get into it enough to be prepared to take the necessary steps to induce the people to vote for you. That is how people usually get into that fantastic assembly.

BROADBENT [*puzzled*] Of course. [*Pause*]. Quite so. [*Pause*]. Er – yes. [*Buoyant again*] I think they will vote for me. Eh? Yes?

AUNT JUDY. Arra why shouldnt they? Look at the people they do vote for!

BROADBENT [*encouraged*] Thats true: thats very true. When I see the windbags, the carpet-baggers, the charlatans, the – the – the fools and ignoramuses who corrupt the multitude by their wealth, or seduce them by spouting balderdash to them, I cannot help thinking that an Englishman with no humbug about him, who will talk straight common sense and take his stand on the solid ground of principle and public duty, must win his way with men of all classes.

KEEGAN [*quietly*] Sir: there was a time, in my ignorant youth, when I should have called you a hypocrite.

BROADBENT [*reddening*] A hypocrite!

NORA [*hastily*] Oh I'm sure you dont think anything of the sort, Mr Keegan.

BROADBENT [*emphatically*] Thank you, Miss Reilly: thank you.

CORNELIUS [*gloomily*] We all have to stretch it a bit in politics: hwats the use o pretendin we dont?

BROADBENT [*stiffly*] I hope I have said or done nothing that calls for any such observation, Mr Doyle. If there is a vice I detest — or against which my whole public life has been a protest — it is the vice of hypocrisy. I would almost rather be inconsistent than insincere.

KEEGAN. Do not be offended, sir: I know that you are quite sincere. There is a saying in the Scripture which runs — so far as the memory of an oldish man can carry the words — Let not the right side of your brain know what the left side doeth. I learnt at Oxford that this is the secret of the Englishman's strange power of making the best of both worlds.

BROADBENT. Surely the text refers to our right and left hands. I am somewhat surprised to hear a member of your Church quote so essentially Protestant a document as the Bible; but at least you might quote it accurately.

LARRY. Tom: with the best intentions youre making an ass of yourself. You dont understand Mr Keegan's peculiar vein of humor.

BROADBENT [*instantly recovering his confidence*] Ah! it was only your delightful Irish humor, Mr Keegan. Of course, of course. How stupid of me! I'm so sorry. [*He pats Keegan consolingly on the back*]. John Bull's wits are still slow, you see. Besides, calling me a hypocrite was too big a joke to swallow all at once, you know.

KEEGAN. You must also allow for the fact that I am mad.

NORA. Ah, dont talk like that, Mr Keegan.

BROADBENT [*encouragingly*] Not at all, not at all. Only a whimsical Irishman, eh?

LARRY. Are you really mad, Mr Keegan?

AUNT JUDY [*shocked*] Oh, Larry, how could you ask him such a thing?

LARRY. I dont think Mr Keegan minds. [*To Keegan*] Whats the true version of the story of that black man you confessed on his deathbed?

KEEGAN. What story have you heard about that?

LARRY. I am informed that when the devil came for the black heathen, he took off your head and turned it three times round before putting it on again; and that your head's been turned ever since.

NORA [*reproachfully*] Larry!

KEEGAN [*blandly*] That is not quite what occurred. [*He collects himself for a serious utterance: they attend involuntarily*]. I heard that a black man was dying, and that the people were afraid to go near him. When I went to the place I found an elderly Hindoo, who told me one of those tales of unmerited misfortune, of cruel ill luck, of relentless persecution by destiny, which sometimes wither the commonplaces of consolation on the lips of a priest. But this man did not complain of his misfortunes. They were brought upon him, he said, by sins committed in a former existence. Then without a word of comfort from me, he died with a clear-eyed resignation that my most earnest exhortations have rarely produced in a Christian, and left me sitting there by his bedside with the mystery of this world suddenly revealed to me.

BROADBENT. That is a remarkable tribute to the liberty of conscience enjoyed by the subjects of our Indian Empire.

LARRY. No doubt; but may we venture to ask what is the mystery of this world?

KEEGAN. This world, sir, is very clearly a place of torment and penance, a place where the fool flourishes and the good and wise are hated and persecuted, a place where men and women torture one another in the name of love; where children are scourged and enslaved in the name of parental duty and education; where the weak in body are poisoned and mutilated in the name of healing, and the weak in character are put to the horrible torture of imprisonment, not for hours but for years, in the name of justice. It is a place where the hardest toil is a welcome refuge from the horror and tedium of pleasure, and where charity and good works are done only for hire to ransom the souls of the spoiler and the sybarite. Now, sir, there is only one place of horror and torment known to my religion; and that place is hell. Therefore it is plain to me that this earth of ours must be hell, and that we are all here, as the Indian revealed to me – perhaps he was sent to reveal it to me – to expiate crimes committed by us in a former existence.

AUNT JUDY [*awestruck*] Heaven save us, what a thing to say!

CORNELIUS [*sighing*] It's a queer world: thats certain.

BROADBENT. Your idea is a very clever one, Mr Keegan: really most brilliant: *I* should never have thought of it. But it seems to me – if I may say so – that you are overlooking the fact that, of the evils you describe, some are absolutely necessary for the preservation of society, and others are encouraged only when the Tories are in office.

LARRY. I expect you were a Tory in a former existence; and that is why you are here.

BROADBENT [*with conviction*] Never, Larry, never. But leaving politics out of the question, I find the world quite good enough for me: rather a jolly place, in fact.

KEEGAN [*looking at him with quiet wonder*] You are satisfied?

BROADBENT. As a reasonable man, yes. I see no evils in the world – except, of course, natural evils – that cannot be remedied by freedom, self-government, and English institutions. I think so, not because I am an Englishman, but as a matter of common sense.

KEEGAN. You feel at home in the world, then?

BROADBENT. Of course. Dont you?

KEEGAN [*from the very depths of his nature*] No.

BROADBENT [*breezily*] Try phosphorus pills. I always take them when my brain is overworked. I'll give you the address in Oxford Street.

KEEGAN [*enigmatically: rising*] Miss Doyle: my wandering fit has come on me: will you excuse me?

AUNT JUDY. To be sure: you know you can come in n nout as you like.

KEEGAN. We can finish the game some other time, Miss Reilly. [*He goes for his hat and stick*].

NORA. No: I'm out with you [*she disarranges the pieces and rises*]. I was too wicked in a former existence to play backgammon with a good man like you.

AUNT JUDY [*whispering to her*] Whisht, whisht, child! Dont set him back on that again.

KEEGAN [*to Nora*] When I look at you, I think that perhaps Ireland is only purgatory, after all. [*He passes on to the garden door*].

NORA. Galong with you!

BROADBENT [*whispering to Cornelius*] Has he a vote?

CORNELIUS [*nodding*] Yes. An theres lotsle vote the way he tells them.

KEEGAN [*at the garden door, with gentle gravity*] Good evening, Mr Broadbent. You hae set me thinking. Thank you.

BROADBENT [*delighted, hurrying across to him to shake hands*] No, really? You find that contact with English ideas is stimulating, eh?

KEEGAN. I am never tired of hearing you talk, Mr Broadbent.

BROADBENT [*modestly remonstrating*] Oh come! come!

KEEGAN. Yes, I assure you. You are an extremely interesting man. [*He goes out*].

BROADBENT [*enthusiastically*] What a nice chap! What an intelligent, broadminded character, considering his cloth! By the way, I'd better have a wash [*He takes up his coat and cap, and leaves the room through the inner door*].

Nora returns to her chair and shuts up the backgammon board.

AUNT JUDY. Keegan's very queer today. He has his mad fit on him.

CORNELIUS [*worried and bitter*] I wouldnt say but he's right after all. It's a contrairy world. [*To Larry*] Why would you be such a fool as to let Broadbent take the seat in parliament from you?

LARRY [*glancing at Nora*] He will take more than that from me before he's done here.

CORNELIUS. I wish he'd never set foot in my house, bad luck to his fat face! D'ye think he'd lend me £300 on the farm, Larry? When I'm so hard up, it seems a waste o money not to mortgage it now it's me own.

LARRY. *I* can lend you £300 on it.

CORNELIUS. No, no; I wasnt putn in for that. When I die and leave you the farm I should like to be able to feel that it was all me own, and not half yours to start with. Now I'll take me oath Barney Doarn's going to ask Broadbent to lend him £500 on the mill to put in a new hweel; for the old one'll harly hol together. An Haffigan cant sleep with covetn that corner o land at the foot of his medda that belongs to Doolan. He'll have to mortgage to buy it. I may as well be first as last. D'ye think Broadbent'd len me a little?

LARRY. I'm quite sure he will.

CORNELIUS. Is he as ready as that? Would he len me five hunderd, d'ye think?

LARRY. He'll lend you more than the landll ever be worth to you; so for Heaven's sake be prudent.

CORNELIUS [*judicially*] All right, all right, me son: I'll be careful. I'm goin into the office for a bit. [*He withdraws through the inner door, obviously to prepare his application to Broadbent*].

AUNT JUDY [*indignantly*] As if he hadnt seen enough o borryin when he was an agent without beginning borryin himself! [*She rises*]. I'll borry him, so I will. [*She puts her knitting on the table and follows him out, with a resolute air that bodes trouble for Cornelius*].

Larry and Nora are left together for the first time since his arrival. She looks at him with a smile that perishes as she sees him aimlessly rocking his chair, and reflecting, evidently not about her, with his lips pursed as if he were whistling. With a catch in her throat she takes up Aunt Judy's knitting, and makes a pretence of going on with it.

NORA. I suppose it didnt seem very long to you.

LARRY [*starting*] Eh? What didnt?

NORA. The eighteen years youve been away.

LARRY. Oh, that! No: it seems hardly more than a week. I've been so busy – had so little time to think.

NORA. Ive had nothing else to do but think.

LARRY. That was very bad for you. Why didnt you give it up? Why did you stay here?

NORA. Because nobody sent for me to go anywhere else, I suppose. Thats why.

LARRY. Yes: one does stick frightfully in the same place, unless some external force comes and routs one out. [*He yawns slightly; but as she looks up quickly at him, he pulls himself together and rises with an air of waking up and setting to work cheerfully to make himself agreeable*]. And how have you been all this time?

NORA. Quite well, thank you.

LARRY. Thats right. [*Suddenly finding that he has nothing else to say, and being ill at ease in consequence, he strolls about the room humming distractedly*].

NORA [*struggling with her tears*] Is that all you have to say to me, Larry?

LARRY. Well, what is there to say? You see, we know each other so well.

NORA [*a little consoled*] Yes: of course we do. [*He does not reply*]. I wonder you came back at all.

LARRY. I couldnt help it. [*She looks up affectionately*]. Tom made me. [*She looks down again quickly to conceal the effect of this blow. He whistles another stave; then resumes*] I had a sort of dread of returning to Ireland. I felt somehow that my luck would turn if I came back. And now here I am, none the worse.

NORA. Praps it's a little dull for you.

LARRY. No: I havnt exhausted the interest of strolling about the old places and remembering and romancing about them.

NORA [*hopefully*] Oh! You do remember the places, then?

LARRY. Of course. They have associations.

NORA [*not doubting that the associations are with her*] I suppose so.

LARRY. M'yes. I can remember particular spots where I had long fits of thinking about the countries I meant to get to when I escaped from Ireland. America and London, and sometimes Rome and the east.

NORA [*deeply mortified*] Was that all you used to be thinking about?

LARRY. Well, there was precious little else to think about here, my dear Nora, except sometimes at sunset, when one got maudlin and called Ireland Erin, and imagined one was remembering the days of old, and so forth. [*He whistles Let Erin Remember*].

NORA. Did jever get a letter I wrote you last February?

LARRY. Oh yes; and I really intended to answer it. But I havnt had a moment; and I knew you wouldnt mind. You see, I am so afraid of boring you by writing about affairs you dont understand and people you dont know! And yet what else have I to write about? I begin a letter; and then I tear it up again. The fact is, fond as we are of one another, Nora, we have so little in common — I mean of course the things one can put in a letter — that correspondence is apt to become the hardest of hard work.

NORA. Yes: it's hard for me to know anything about you if you never tell me anything.

LARRY [*pettishly*] Nora: a man cant sit down and write his life day by day when he's tired enough with having lived it.

NORA. I'm not blaming you.

LARRY [*looking at her with some concern*] You seem rather out of spirits. [*Going closer to her, anxiously and tenderly*] You havnt got neuralgia, have you?

NORA. No.

LARRY [*reassured*] I get a touch of it sometimes when I am below par.

[*Absently, again strolling about*] Yes, yes. [*He gazes through the doorway at the Irish landscape, and sings, almost unconsciously, but very expressively, an air from Offenbach's Whittington*].

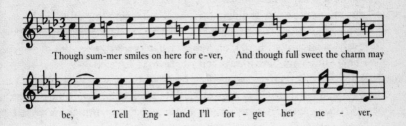

Though sum-mer smiles on here for e-ver,   And though full sweet the charm may

be,   Tell Eng-land I'll for-get her   ne - ver,

[*Nora, who has been at first touched by the tenderness of his singing, puts down her knitting at this very unexpected sentiment, and stares at him. He continues until the melody soars out of his range, when he trails off into whistling Let Erin Remember*].

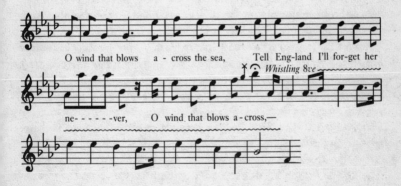

O wind that blows   a - cross the sea,   Tell Eng-land I'll for-get her

ne - - - - - ver,   O wind that blows a-cross,—

I'm afraid I'm boring you, Nora, though youre too kind to say so.

NORA. Are you wanting to get back to England already?

LARRY. Not at all. Not at all.

NORA. Thats a queer song to sing to me if youre not.

LARRY. The song! Oh, it doesnt mean anything: it's by a German Jew, like most English patriotic sentiment. Never mind me, my dear: go on with your work; and dont let me bore you.

NORA [*bitterly*] Rosscullen isnt such a lively place that I am likely to be bored by you at our first talk together after eighteen years, though you dont seem to have much to say to me after all.

LARRY. Eighteen years is a devilish long time, Nora. Now if it had been eighteen minutes, or even eighteen months, we should be able to pick up the interrupted thread, and chatter like two magpies. But as it is, I have simply nothing to say; and you seem to have less.

NORA. I – [*her tears choke her; but she keeps up appearances desperately*].

LARRY [*quite unconscious of his cruelty*] In a week or so we shall be quite old friends again. Meanwhile, as I feel that I am not making myself particularly entertaining, I'll take myself off. Tell Tom Ive gone for a stroll over the hill.

NORA. You seem very fond of Tom, as you call him.

LARRY [*the triviality going suddenly out of his voice*] Yes: I'm fond of Tom.

NORA. Oh, well, dont let me keep you from him.

LARRY. I know quite well that my departure will be a relief. Rather a failure, this first meeting after eighteen years, eh? Well, never mind: these great sentimental events always are failures; and now the worst of it's over anyhow. [*He goes out through the garden door*].

Nora, left alone, struggles wildly to save herself from breaking down, and then drops her face on the table and gives way to a convulsion of crying. Her sobs shake her so that she can hear nothing; and she has no suspicion that she is no longer alone until her head and breast are raised by Broadbent who, returning newly washed and combed through the inner door, has seen her condition, first with surprise and concern, and then with an emotional disturbance that quite upsets him.

BROADBENT. Miss Reilly. Miss Reilly. Whats the matter? Dont cry: I cant stand it: you mustnt cry. [*She makes a choked effort to speak, so painful that he continues with impulsive sympathy*] No: dont try to speak: it's all right now. Have your cry out: never mind me: trust me. [*Gathering her to him, and babbling consolatorily*] Cry on my chest: the only really comfortable place for a woman to cry is a man's chest: a real man, a real friend. A good broad chest, eh? not less than forty-two inches – no: dont fuss: never mind the conventions: we're two friends, arnt we? Come now, come, come! It's all right and comfortable and happy now, isnt it?

NORA [*through her tears*] Let me go. I want me hankerchief.

BROADBENT [*holding her with one arm and producing a large silk handkerchief from his breast pocket*] Heres a handkerchief. Let me [*he dabs her tears dry with it*]. Never mind your own: it's too small: it's one of those wretched little cambric handkerchiefs —

NORA [*sobbing*] Indeed it's a common cotton one.

BROADBENT. Of course it's a common cotton one — silly little cotton one — not good enough for the dear eyes of Nora Cryna —

NORA [*spluttering into a hysterical laugh and clutching him convulsively with her fingers while she tries to stifle her laughter against his collar bone*] Oh dont make me laugh: please dont make me laugh.

BROADBENT [*terrified*] I didnt mean to, on my soul. What is it? What is it?

NORA. Nora Creena, Nora Creena.

BROADBENT [*patting her*] Yes, yes, of course, Nora Creena, Nora acushla [*he makes cush rhyme to plush*] —

NORA. Acushla [*she makes cush rhyme to bush*].

BROADBENT. Oh, confound the language! Nora darling — my Nora — the Nora I love —

NORA [*shocked into propriety*] You mustnt talk like that to me.

BROADBENT [*suddenly becoming prodigiously solemn and letting her go*] No, of course not. I dont mean it. At least I do mean it, but I know it's premature. I had no right to take advantage of your being a little upset; but I lost my self-control for a moment.

NORA [*wondering at him*] I think youre a very kind-hearted man, Mr Broadbent; but you seem to me to have no self-control at all [*she turns her face away with a keen pang of shame and adds*] no more than myself.

BROADBENT [*resolutely*] Oh yes, I have: you should see me when I am really roused: then I have TREMENDOUS self-control. Remember: we have been alone together only once before; and then, I regret to say, I was in a disgusting state.

NORA. Ah no, Mr Broadbent: you wernt disgusting.

BROADBENT [*mercilessly*] Yes I was: nothing can excuse it: perfectly beastly. It must have made a most unfavorable impression on you.

NORA. Oh, sure it's all right. Say no more about that.

BROADBENT. I must, Miss Reilly: it is my duty. I shall not detain you long. May I ask you to sit down. [*He indicates her chair with oppressive solemnity. She sits down wondering. He then, with the same portentous gravity, places a chair for himself near her; sits down; and proceeds to explain*]. First, Miss Reilly, may I say that I have tasted nothing of an alcoholic nature today.

NORA. It doesnt seem to make as much difference in you as it would in an Irishman, somehow.

BROADBENT. Perhaps not. Perhaps not. I never quite lose myself.

NORA [*consolingly*] Well, anyhow, youre all right now.

BROADBENT [*fervently*] Thank you, Miss Reilly: I am. Now we shall get along. [*Tenderly, lowering his voice*] Nora: I was in earnest last night. [*Nora moves as if to rise*]. No: one moment. You must not think I am going to press you for an answer before you have known me for 24 hours. I am a reasonable man, I hope; and I am prepared to wait as long as you like, provided you will give me some small assurance that the answer will not be unfavorable.

NORA. How could I go back from it if I did? I sometimes think youre not quite right in your head, Mr Broadbent, you say such funny things.

BROADBENT. Yes: I know I have a strong sense of humor which sometimes makes people doubt whether I am quite serious. That is why I have always thought I should like to marry an Irishwoman. She would always understand my jokes. For instance, you would understand them, eh?

NORA [*uneasily*] Mr Broadbent: I couldnt.

BROADBENT [*soothingly*] Wait: let me break this to you gently, Miss Reilly: hear me out. I daresay you have noticed that in speaking to you I have been putting a very strong constraint on myself, so as to avoid wounding your delicacy by too abrupt an avowal of my feelings. Well, I feel now that the time has come to be open, to be frank, to be explicit. Miss Reilly: you have inspired in me a very strong attachment. Perhaps, with a woman's intuition, you have already guessed that.

NORA [*rising distractedly*] Why do you talk to me in that unfeeling nonsensical way?

BROADBENT [*rising also, much astonished*] Unfeeling! Nonsensical!

NORA. Dont you know that you have said things to me that no man ought to say unless – unless – [*she suddenly breaks down again and hides her face on the table as before*] Oh, go away from me: I wont get married at all: what is it but heartbreak and disappointment?

BROADBENT [*developing the most formidable symptoms of rage and grief*] Do you mean to say that you are going to refuse me? that you dont care for me?

NORA [*looking at him in consternation*] Oh, dont take it to heart, Mr Br—

BROADBENT [*flushed and almost choking*] I dont want to be petted and blarneyed. [*With childish rage*] I love you. I want you for my wife. [*In despair*] I cant help your refusing. I'm helpless: I can do nothing. You have no right to ruin my whole life. You – [*a hysterical convulsion stops him*].

NORA [*almost awestruck*] Youre not going to cry, are you? I never thought a man could cry. Dont.

BROADBENT. I'm not crying. I – I – I leave that sort of thing to your damned sentimental Irishmen. You think I have no feeling because I am a plain unemotional Englishman, with no powers of expression.

NORA. I dont think you know the sort of man you are at all. Whatever may be the matter with you, it's not want of feeling.

BROADBENT [*hurt and petulant*] It's you who have no feeling. Youre as heartless as Larry.

NORA. What do you expect me to do? Is it to throw meself at your head the minute the word is out o your mouth?

BROADBENT [*striking his silly head with his fists*] Oh, what a fool! what a brute I am! It's only your Irish delicacy: of course, of course. You mean Yes. Eh? What? Yes? yes? yes?

NORA. I think you might understand that though I might choose to be an old maid, I could never marry anybody but you now.

BROADBENT [*clasping her violently to his breast, with a crow of immense relief and triumph*] Ah, thats right, thats right: thats magnificent. I knew you would see what a first-rate thing this will be for both of us.

NORA [*incommoded and not at all enraptured by his ardor*] Youre dreadfully strong, an a gradle too free with your strength. An I never thought o whether it'd be a good thing for us or not. But when you found me here that time, I let you be kind to me, and cried in your arms, because I was too wretched to think of anything but the comfort of it. And how could I let any other man touch me after that?

BROADBENT [*moved*] Now thats very nice of you, Nora: thats really most delicately womanly [*he kisses her hand chivalrously*].

NORA [*looking earnestly and a little doubtfully at him*] Surely if you let one woman cry on you like that youd never let another touch you.

BROADBENT [*conscientiously*] One should not. One ought not, my dear girl. But the honest truth is, if a chap is at all a pleasant sort of chap, his chest becomes a fortification that has to stand many assaults: at least it is so in England.

NORA [*curtly, much disgusted*] Then youd better marry an Englishwoman.

BROADBENT [*making a wry face*] No, no: the Englishwoman is too prosaic for my taste, too material, too much of the animated beefsteak about her. The ideal is what I like. Now Larry's taste is just the opposite: he likes em solid and bouncing and rather keen about him. It's a very convenient difference; for weve never been in love with the same woman.

NORA. An d'ye mean to tell me to me face that youve ever been in love before?

BROADBENT. Lord! yes.

NORA. I'm not your first love!

BROADBENT. First love is only a little foolishness and a lot of curiosity: no really self-respecting woman would take advantage of it. No, my dear Nora: Ive done with all that long ago. Love affairs always end in rows. We're not going to have any rows: we're going to have a solid four-square home: man and wife: comfort and common sense. And plenty of affection, eh [*he puts his arm round her with confident proprietorship*]?

NORA [*coldly, trying to get away*] I dont want any other woman's leavings.

BROADBENT [*holding her*] Nobody asked you to, maam. I never asked any woman to marry me before.

NORA [*severely*] Then why didnt you if youre an honorable man?

BROADBENT. Well, to tell you the truth, they were mostly married already. But never mind! there was nothing wrong. Come! dont take a mean advantage of me. After all, you must have had a fancy or two yourself, eh?

NORA [*conscience-stricken*] Yes. I suppose Ive no right to be particular.

BROADBENT [*humbly*] I know I'm not good enough for you, Nora. But no man is, you know, when the woman is a really nice woman.

NORA. Oh, I'm no better than yourself. I may as well tell you about it.

BROADBENT. No, no: lets have no telling: much better not. *I* shant tell you anything: dont you tell me anything. Perfect confidence in one another and no tellings: thats the way to avoid rows.

NORA. Dont think it was anything I need be ashamed of.

BROADBENT. I dont.

NORA. It was only that I'd never known anybody else that I could care for; and I was foolish enough once to think that Larry –

BROADBENT [*disposing of the idea at once*] Larry! Oh, that wouldnt have done at all, not at all. You dont know Larry as I do, my dear. He has absolutely no capacity for enjoyment: he couldnt make any woman happy. He's as clever as be-blowed; but life's too earthly for him: he doesnt really care for anything or anybody.

NORA. I've found that out.

BROADBENT. Of course you have. No, my dear: take my word for it, youre jolly well out of that. There! [*swinging her round against his breast*] thats much more comfortable for you.

NORA [*with Irish peevishness*] Ah, you mustnt go on like that. I dont like it.

BROADBENT [*unabashed*] Youll acquire the taste by degrees. You mustnt mind me: it's an absolute necessity of my nature that I should have somebody to hug occasionally. Besides, it's good for you: itll plump out your muscles and make em elastic and set up your figure.

NORA. Well, I'm sure! if this is English manners! Arnt you ashamed to talk about such things?

BROADBENT [*in the highest feather*] Not a bit. By George, Nora, it's a tremendous thing to be able to enjoy oneself. Lets go off for a walk out of this stuffy little room. I want the open air to expand in. Come along. Co-o-ome along. [*He puts her arm into his and sweeps her out into the garden as an equinoctial gale might sweep a dry leaf*].

Later in the evening, the grasshopper is again enjoying the sunset by the great stone on the hill; but this time he enjoys neither the stimulus of Keegan's conversation nor the pleasure of terrifying Patsy Farrell. He is alone until Nora and Broadbent come up the hill arm in arm. Broadbent is still breezy and confident; but she has her head averted from him and is almost in tears.

BROADBENT [*stopping to snuff up the hillside air*] Ah! I like this spot.

I like this view. This would be a jolly good place for a hotel and a golf links. Friday to Tuesday, railway ticket and hotel all inclusive. I tell you, Nora, I'm going to develop this place. [*Looking at her*] Hallo! Whats the matter? Tired?

NORA [*unable to restrain her tears*] I'm ashamed out o me life.

BROADBENT [*astonished*] Ashamed! What of?

NORA. Oh, how could you drag me all round the place like that, telling everybody that we're going to be married, and introjoocing me to the lowest of the low, and letting them shake hans with me, and encouraging them to make free with us? I little thought I should live to be shaken hans with be Doolan in broad daylight in the public street of Rosscullen.

BROADBENT. But, my dear, Doolan's a publican: a most influential man. By the way, I asked him if his wife would be at home tomorrow. He said she would; so you must take the motor car round and call on her.

NORA [*aghast*] Is it me call on Doolan's wife!

BROADBENT. Yes, of course: call on all their wives. We must get a copy of the register and a supply of canvassing cards. No use calling on people who havnt votes. Youll be a great success as a canvasser, Nora: they call you the heiress; and theyll be flattered no end by your calling, especially as youve never cheapened yourself by speaking to them before – have you?

NORA [*indignantly*] Not likely, indeed.

BROADBENT. Well, we mustnt be stiff and stand-off, you know. We must be thoroughly democratic, and patronize everybody without distinction of class. I tell you I'm a jolly lucky man, Nora Cryna. I get engaged to the most delightful woman in Ireland; and it turns out that I couldnt have done a smarter stroke of electioneering.

NORA. An would you let me demean meself like that, just to get yourself into parliament?

BROADBENT [*buoyantly*] Aha! Wait till you find out what an exciting game electioneering is: youll be mad to get me in. Besides, youd like people to say that Tom Broadbent's wife had been the making of him? that she got him into parliament? into the Cabinet, perhaps, eh?

NORA. God knows I dont grudge you me money! But to lower meself to the level of common people –

BROADBENT. To a member's wife, Nora, nobody is common provided he's on the register. Come, my dear! it's all right: do you think I'd let you do it if it wasnt? The best people do it. Everybody does it.

NORA [*who has been biting her lip and looking over the hill, disconsolate and unconvinced*] Well, praps you know best what they do in England. They must have very little respect for themselves. I think I'll go in now. I see Larry and Mr Keegan coming up the hill; and I'm not fit to talk to them.

BROADBENT. Just wait and say something nice to Keegan. They tell me he controls nearly as many votes as Father Dempsey himself.

NORA. You little know Peter Keegan. He'd see through me as if I was a pane o glass.

BROADBENT. Oh, he wont like it any the less for that. What really flatters a man is that you think him worth flattering. Not that I would flatter any man: dont think that. I'll just go and meet him. [*He goes down the hill with the eager forward look of a man about to greet a valued acquaintance. Nora dries her eyes, and turns to go as Larry strolls up the hill to her*].

LARRY. Nora. [*She turns and looks at him hardly, without a word. He continues anxiously, in his most conciliatory tone*]. When I left you that time, I was just as wretched as you. I didnt rightly know what I wanted to say; and my tongue kept clacking to cover the loss I was at. Well, Ive been thinking ever since; and now I know what I ought to have said. Ive come back to say it.

NORA. Youve come too late, then. You thought eighteen years was not long enough, and that you might keep me waiting a day longer. Well, you were mistaken. I'm engaged to your friend Mr Broadbent; and I'm done with you.

LARRY [*naïvely*] But that was the very thing I was going to advise you to do.

NORA [*involuntarily*] Oh you brute! to tell me that to me face!

LARRY [*nervously relapsing into his most Irish manner*] Nora, dear, dont you understand that I'm an Irishman, and he's an Englishman. He wants you; and he grabs you. *I* want you; and I quarrel with you and have to go on wanting you.

NORA. So you may. Youd better go back to England to the animated beefsteaks youre so fond of.

LARRY [*amazed*] Nora! [*Guessing where she got the metaphor*] He's been talking of me, I see. Well, never mind: we must be friends, you and I. I dont want his marriage to you to be his divorce from me.

NORA. You care more for him than you ever did for me.

LARRY [*with curt sincerity*] Yes of course I do: why should I tell you lies about it? Nora Reilly was a person of very little consequence to me or anyone else outside this miserable little hole. But Mrs Tom Broadbent will be a person of very considerable consequence indeed. Play your new part well, and there will be no more neglect, no more loneliness, no more idle regrettings and vain-hopings in the evenings by the Round Tower, but real life and real work and real cares and real joys among real people: solid English life in London, the very centre of the world. You will find your work cut out for you keeping Tom's house and entertaining Tom's friends and getting Tom into parliament; but it will be worth the effort.

NORA. You talk as if I was under obligation to him for marrying me.

LARRY. I talk as I think. Youve made a very good match, let me tell you.

NORA. Indeed! Well, some people might say he's not done so badly himself.

LARRY. If you mean that you will be a treasure to him, he thinks so now; and you can keep him thinking so if you like.

NORA. I wasnt thinking o meself at all.

LARRY. Were you thinking of your money, Nora?

NORA. I didnt say so.

LARRY. Your money will not pay your cook's wages in London.

NORA [*flaming up*] If thats true – and the more shame for you to throw it in me face if it is true – at all events itll make us independent; for if the worst comes to the worst, we can always come back here and live on it. An if I have to keep his house for him, at all events I can keep you out of it; for Ive done with you; and I wish I'd never seen you. So goodbye to you, Mister Larry Doyle. [*She turns her back on him and goes home*].

LARRY [*watching her as she goes*] Goodbye. Goodbye. Oh, thats so Irish! Irish both of us to the backbone: Irish! Irish! Iri—

Broadbent arrives, conversing energetically with Keegan.

BROADBENT. Nothing pays like a golfing hotel, if you hold the land instead of the shares, and if the furniture people stand in with you, and if you are a good man of business.

LARRY. Nora's gone home.

BROADBENT [*with conviction*] You were right this morning, Larry. I must feed up Nora. She's weak; and it makes her fanciful. Oh, by the way, did I tell you that we're engaged?

LARRY. She told me herself.

BROADBENT [*complacently*] She's rather full of it, as you may imagine. Poor Nora! Well, Mr Keegan, as I said, I begin to see my way here. I begin to see my way.

KEEGAN [*with a courteous inclination*] The conquering Englishman, sir. Within 24 hours of your arrival you have carried off our only heiress, and practically secured the parliamentary seat. And you have promised me that when I come here in the evenings to meditate on my madness; to watch the shadow of the Round Tower lengthening in the sunset; to break my heart uselessly in the curtained gloaming over the dead heart and blinded soul of the island of the saints, you will comfort me with the bustle of a great hotel, and the sight of the little children carrying the golf clubs of your tourists as a preparation for the life to come.

BROADBENT [*quite touched, mutely offering him a cigar to console him, at which he smiles and shakes his head*] Yes, Mr Keegan: youre quite right. Theres poetry in everything, even [*looking absently into the cigar case*] in the most modern prosaic things, if you know how to extract it [*he extracts a cigar for himself and offers one to Larry, who takes it*]. If I was to be shot for it I couldnt extract it myself; but thats where you come in, you see. [*Roguishly, waking up from his reverie and bustling Keegan goodhumoredly*] And then *I* shall wake you up a bit. Thats where *I* come in: eh? d'ye see? Eh? eh? [*He pats him very pleasantly on the shoulder, half admiringly, half pityingly*]. Just so, just so. [*Coming back to business*] By the way, I believe I can do better than a light railway here. There seems to be no question now that the motor boat has come to stay. Well, look at your magnificent river there, going to waste.

KEEGAN [*closing his eyes*]

'Silent, O Moyle, be the roar of thy waters.'

BROADBENT. You know, the roar of a motor boat is quite pretty.

KEEGAN. Provided it does not drown the Angelus.

BROADBENT [*reassuringly*] Oh no: it wont do that: not the least danger. You know, a church bell can make a devil of a noise when it likes.

KEEGAN. You have an answer for everything, sir. But your plans leave one question still unanswered: how to get butter out of a dog's throat.

BROADBENT. Eh?

KEEGAN. You cannot build your golf links and hotels in the air. For that you must own our land. And how will you drag our acres from the ferret's grip of Matthew Haffigan? How will you persuade Cornelius Doyle to forgo the pride of being a small landowner? How will Barney Doran's millrace agree with your motor boats? Will Doolan help you to get a licence for your hotel?

BROADBENT. My dear sir: to all intents and purposes the syndicate I represent already owns half Rosscullen. Doolan's is a tied house; and the brewers are in the syndicate. As to Haffigan's farm and Doran's mill and Mr Doyle's place and half a dozen others, they will be mortgaged to me before a month is out.

KEEGAN. But pardon me, you will not lend them more on their land than the land is worth; so they will be able to pay you the interest.

BROADBENT. Ah, you are a poet, Mr Keegan, not a man of business.

LARRY. We will lend every one of these men half as much again on their land as it is worth, or ever can be worth, to them.

BROADBENT. You forget, sir, that we, with our capital, our knowledge, our organization, and may I say our English business habits, can make or lose ten pounds out of land that Haffigan, with all his industry, could not make or lose ten shillings out of. Doran's mill is a superannuated folly: I shall want it for electric lighting.

LARRY. What is the use of giving land to such men? they are too small, too poor, too ignorant, too simpleminded to hold it against us: you might as well give a dukedom to a crossing sweeper.

BROADBENT. Yes, Mr Keegan: this place may have an industrial future, or it may have a residential future: I cant tell yet; but it's not going to be a future in the hands of your Dorans and Haffigans, poor devils!

KEEGAN. It may have no future at all. Have you thought of that?

BROADBENT. Oh, I'm not afraid of that. I have faith in Ireland. Great faith, Mr Keegan.

KEEGAN. And we have none: only empty enthusiasms and patriotisms, and emptier memories and regrets. Ah yes: you have some excuse for believing that if there be any future, it will be yours; for our faith seems dead, and our hearts cold and cowed. An island of dreamers who wake up in your jails, of critics and cowards whom you buy and tame for your own service, of bold rogues who help you to plunder us that they may plunder you afterwards.

BROADBENT [*a little impatient of this unbusinesslike view*] Yes, yes; but you know you might say that of any country. The fact is, there are only two qualities in the world: efficiency and inefficiency, and only two sorts of people: the efficient and the inefficient. It dont matter whether theyre English or Irish. I shall collar this place, not because I'm an Englishman and Haffigan and Co are Irishmen, but because theyre duffers, and I know my way about.

KEEGAN. Have you considered what is to become of Haffigan?

LARRY. Oh, we'll employ him in some capacity or other, and probably pay him more than he makes for himself now.

BROADBENT [*dubiously*] Do you think so? No no: Haffigan's too old. It really doesnt pay now to take on men over forty even for unskilled labor, which I suppose is all Haffigan would be good for. No: Haffigan had better go to America, or into the Union, poor old chap! He's worked out, you know: you can see it.

KEEGAN. Poor lost soul, so cunningly fenced in with invisible bars!

LARRY. Haffigan doesnt matter much. He'll die presently.

BROADBENT [*shocked*] Oh come, Larry! Dont be unfeeling. It's hard on Haffigan. It's always hard on the inefficient.

LARRY. Pah! what does it matter where an old and broken man spends his last days, or whether he has a million at the bank or only the workhouse dole? It's the young men, the able men, that matter. The real tragedy of Haffigan is the tragedy of his wasted youth, his stunted mind, his drudging over his clods and pigs until he has become a clod and a pig himself – until the soul within him has smouldered into nothing but a dull temper that hurts himself and all around him. I say let him die, and let us have no more of his like. And let young Ireland take care that it doesnt share his fate, instead of making another empty grievance of it. Let your syndicate come –

BROADBENT. Your syndicate too, old chap. You have your bit of the stock.

LARRY. Yes: mine if you like. Well, our syndicate has no conscience:

it has no more regard for your Haffigans and Doolans and Dorans than it has for a gang of Chinese coolies. It will use your patriotic blatherskite and balderdash to get parliamentary powers over you as cynically as it would bait a mousetrap with toasted cheese. It will plan, and organize, and find capital while you slave like bees for it and revenge yourselves by paying politicians and penny newspapers out of your small wages to write articles and report speeches against its wickedness and tyranny, and to crack up your own Irish heroism, just as Haffigan once paid a witch a penny to put a spell on Billy Byrne's cow. In the end it will grind the nonsense out of you, and grind strength and sense into you.

BROADBENT [*out of patience*] Why cant you say a simple thing simply, Larry, without all that Irish exaggeration and talky-talky? The syndicate is a perfectly respectable body of responsible men of good position. We'll take Ireland in hand, and by straightforward business habits teach it efficiency and self-help on sound Liberal principles. You agree with me, Mr Keegan, dont you?

KEEGAN. Sir: I may even vote for you.

BROADBENT [*sincerely moved, shaking his hand warmly*] You shall never regret it, Mr Keegan: I give you my word for that. I shall bring money here: I shall raise wages: I shall found public institutions: a library, a Polytechnic (undenominational, of course), a gymnasium, a cricket club, perhaps an art school. I shall make a Garden City of Rosscullen: the Round Tower shall be thoroughly repaired and restored.

KEEGAN. And our place of torment shall be as clean and orderly as the cleanest and most orderly place I know in Ireland, which is our poetically named Mountjoy prison. Well, perhaps I had better vote for an efficient devil that knows his own mind and his own business than for a foolish patriot who has no mind and no business.

BROADBENT [*stiffly*] Devil is rather a strong expression in that connection, Mr Keegan.

KEEGAN. Not from a man who knows that this world is hell. But since the word offends you, let me soften it, and compare you simply to an ass. [*Larry whitens with anger*].

BROADBENT [*reddening*] An ass!

KEEGAN [*gently*] You may take it without offence from a madman who calls the ass his brother – and a very honest, useful and faithful brother, too. The ass, sir, is the most efficient of beasts, matter-of-fact, hardy, friendly when you treat him as a fellow-creature, stubborn when you abuse him, ridiculous only in love, which sets him braying, and in politics, which move him to roll about in the public road and raise a dust about nothing. Can you deny these qualities and habits in yourself, sir?

BROADBENT [*goodhumoredly*] Well, yes, I'm afraid I do, you know.

KEEGAN. Then perhaps you will confess to the ass's one fault.

BROADBENT. Perhaps so: what is it?

KEEGAN. That he wastes all his virtues – his efficiency, as you call it – in doing the will of his greedy masters instead of doing the will of Heaven that is in himself. He is efficient in the service of Mammon, mighty in mischief, skilful in ruin, heroic in destruction. But he comes to browse here without knowing that the soil his hoof touches is holy ground. Ireland, sir, for good or evil, is like no other place under heaven; and no man can touch its sod or breathe its air without becoming better or worse. It produces two kinds of men in strange perfection: saints and traitors. It is called the island of the saints; but indeed in these later years it might be more fitly called the island of the traitors; for our harvest of these is the fine flower of the world's crop of infamy. But the day may come when these islands shall live by the quality of their men rather than by the abundance of their minerals; and then we shall see.

LARRY. Mr Keegan: if you are going to be sentimental about Ireland, I shall bid you good evening. We have had enough of that, and more than enough of cleverly proving that everybody who is not an Irishman is an ass. It is neither good sense nor good manners. It will not stop the syndicate; and it will not interest young Ireland so much as my friend's gospel of efficiency.

BROADBENT. Ah, yes, yes: efficiency is the thing. I dont in the least mind your chaff, Mr Keegan; but Larry's right on the main point. The world belongs to the efficient.

KEEGAN [*with polished irony*] I stand rebuked, gentlemen. But believe me, I do every justice to the efficiency of you and your syndicate. You are both, I am told, thoroughly efficient civil engineers; and I have no doubt the golf links will be a triumph of your art. Mr Broadbent will get into parliament most efficiently, which is more than St Patrick

could do if he were alive now. You may even build the hotel efficiently
if you can find enough efficient masons, carpenters, and plumbers,
which I rather doubt. [*Dropping his irony, and beginning to fall into
the attitude of the priest rebuking sin*] When the hotel becomes insolvent
[*Broadbent takes his cigar out of his mouth, a little taken aback*] your
English business habits will secure the thorough efficiency of the
liquidation. You will reorganize the scheme efficiently; you will
liquidate its second bankruptcy efficiently [*Broadbent and Larry look
quickly at one another; for this, unless the priest is an old financial hand,
must be inspiration*]; you will get rid of its original shareholders
efficiently after efficiently ruining them; and you will finally profit
very efficiently by getting that hotel for a few shillings in the pound.
[*More and more sternly*] Besides these efficient operations, you will
foreclose your mortgages most efficiently [*his rebuking forefinger goes
up in spite of himself*]; you will drive Haffigan to America very
efficiently; you will find a use for Barney Doran's foul mouth and
bullying temper by employing him to slave-drive your laborers very
efficiently; and [*low and bitter*] when at last this poor desolate country-
side becomes a busy mint in which we shall all slave to make money
for you, with our Polytechnic to teach us how to do it efficiently, and
our library to fuddle the few imaginations your distilleries will spare,
and our repaired Round Tower with admission sixpence, and refresh-
ments and penny-in-the-slot mutoscopes to make it interesting, then
no doubt your English and American shareholders will spend all the
money we make for them very efficiently in shooting and hunting,
in operations for cancer and appendicitis, in gluttony and gambling;
and you will devote what they save to fresh land development schemes.
For four wicked centuries the world has dreamed this foolish dream
of efficiency; and the end is not yet. But the end will come.

BROADBENT [*seriously*] Too true, Mr Keegan, only too true. And most
eloquently put. It reminds me of poor Ruskin: a great man, you know.
I sympathize. Believe me, I'm on your side. Dont sneer, Larry: I used
to read a lot of Shelley years ago. Let us be faithful to the dreams
of our youth [*he wafts a wreath of cigar smoke at large across the hill*].

KEEGAN. Come, Mr Doyle! is this English sentiment so much more
efficient than our Irish sentiment, after all? Mr Broadbent spends his
life inefficiently admiring the thoughts of great men, and efficiently

serving the cupidity of base money hunters. We spend our lives efficiently sneering at him and doing nothing. Which of us has any right to reproach the other?

BROADBENT [*coming down the hill again to Keegan's right hand*] But you know, something must be done.

KEEGAN. Yes: when we cease to do, we cease to live. Well, what shall we do?

BROADBENT. Why, what lies to our hand.

KEEGAN. Which is the making of golf links and hotels to bring idlers to a country which workers have left in millions because it is a hungry land, a naked land, an ignorant and oppressed land.

BROADBENT. But, hang it all, the idlers will bring money from England to Ireland!

KEEGAN. Just as our idlers have for so many generations taken money from Ireland to England. Has that saved England from poverty and degradation more horrible than we have ever dreamed of? When I went to England, sir, I hated England. Now I pity it. [*Broadbent can hardly conceive an Irishman pitying England; but as Larry intervenes angrily, he gives it up and takes to the hill and his cigar again*].

LARRY. Much good your pity will do it!

KEEGAN. In the accounts kept in heaven, Mr Doyle, a heart purified of hatred may be worth more than even a Land Development Syndicate of Anglicized Irishmen and Gladstonized Englishmen.

LARRY. Oh, in heaven, no doubt. I have never been there. Can you tell me where it is?

KEEGAN. Could you have told me this morning where hell is? Yet you know now that it is here. Do not despair of finding heaven: it may be no farther off.

LARRY [*ironically*] On this holy ground, as you call it, eh?

KEEGAN [*with fierce intensity*] Yes, perhaps, even on this holy ground which such Irishmen as you have turned into a Land of Derision.

BROADBENT [*coming between them*] Take care! you will be quarrelling presently. Oh, you Irishmen, you Irishmen! Toujours Ballyhooly, eh? [*Larry, with a shrug, half comic, half impatient, turns away up the hill, but presently strolls back on Keegan's right. Broadbent adds, confidentially to Keegan*] Stick to the Englishman, Mr Keegan: he has a bad name here; but at least he can forgive you for being an Irishman.

KEEGAN. Sir: when you speak to me of English and Irish you forget that I am a Catholic. My country is not Ireland nor England, but the whole mighty realm of my Church. For me there are but two countries: heaven and hell; but two conditions of men: salvation and damnation. Standing here between you the Englishman, so clever in your foolishness, and this Irishman, so foolish in his cleverness, I cannot in my ignorance be sure which of you is the more deeply damned; but I should be unfaithful to my calling if I opened the gates of my heart less widely to one than to the other.

LARRY. In either case it would be an impertinence, Mr Keegan, as your approval is not of the slightest consequence to us. What use do you suppose all this drivel is to men with serious practical business in hand?

BROADBENT. I dont agree with that, Larry. I think these things cannot be said too often: they keep up the moral tone of the community. As you know, I claim the right to think for myself in religious matters: in fact, I am ready to avow myself a bit of a – of a – well, I dont care who knows it – a bit of a Unitarian; but if the Church of England contained a few men like Mr Keegan, I should certainly join it.

KEEGAN. You do me too much honor, sir. [*With priestly humility to Larry*] Mr Doyle: I am to blame for having unintentionally set your mind somewhat on edge against me. I beg your pardon.

LARRY [*unimpressed and hostile*] I didnt stand on ceremony with you; you neednt stand on it with me. Fine manners and fine words are cheap in Ireland: you can keep both for my friend here, who is still imposed on by them. *I* know their value.

KEEGAN. You mean you dont know their value.

LARRY [*angrily*] I mean what I say.

KEEGAN [*turning quietly to the Englishman*] You see, Mr Broadbent, I only make the hearts of my countrymen harder when I preach to them: the gates of hell still prevail against me. I shall wish you good evening. I am better alone, at the Round Tower, dreaming of heaven. [*He goes up the hill*].

LARRY. Aye, thats it! there you are! dreaming! dreaming! dreaming! dreaming!

KEEGAN [*halting and turning to them for the last time*] Every dream is a prophecy: every jest is an earnest in the womb of Time.

BROADBENT [*reflectively*] Once, when I was a small kid, I dreamt I was in heaven. [*They both stare at him*]. It was a sort of pale blue satin place, with all the pious old ladies in our congregation sitting as if they were at a service; and there was some awful person in the study at the other side of the hall. I didnt enjoy it, you know. What is it like in your dreams?

KEEGAN. In my dreams it is a country where the State is the Church and the Church the people: three in one and one in three. It is a commonwealth in which work is play and play is life: three in one and one in three. It is a temple in which the priest is the worshipper and the worshipper the worshipped: three in one and one in three. It is a godhead in which all life is human and all humanity divine: three in one and one in three. It is, in short, the dream of a madman. [*He goes away across the hill*].

BROADBENT [*looking after him affectionately*] What a regular old Church and State Tory he is! He's a character: he'll be an attraction here. Really almost equal to Ruskin and Carlyle.

LARRY. Yes; and much good they did with all their talk!

BROADBENT. Oh tut, tut, Larry! They improved my mind: they raised my tone enormously. I feel sincerely obliged to Keegan: he has made me feel a better man: distinctly better. [*With sincere elevation*] I feel now as I never did before that I am right in devoting my life to the cause of Ireland. Come along and help me to choose the site for the hotel.

To the Audience
at the Kingsway Theatre

A Personal Appeal from the Author of
John Bull's Other Island

Dear Sir or Madam,

It is your custom to receive my plays with the most generous and unrestrained applause. You sometimes compel the performers to pause at the end of every line until your laughter has quieted down. I am not ungrateful; but may I ask you a few questions?

Are you aware that you would get out of the Theatre half an hour earlier if you listened to the play in silence and did not applaud until the fall of the curtain?

Do you really consider that a performance is improved by continual interruptions, however complimentary they may be to the actors and the author?

Do you not think that the naturalness of the pre-presentation must be destroyed, and therefore your own pleasure greatly diminished, when the audience insists on taking part in it by shouts of applause and laughter, and the actors have repeatedly to stop acting until the noise is over?

Have you considered that in all good plays tears and laughter lie very close together, and that it must be very distressing to an actress who is trying to keep her imagination fixed on pathetic emotions to hear bursts of laughter breaking out at something she is supposed to be unconscious of?

Do you know that even when there is no such conflict of comic and tragic on the stage, the strain of performing is greatly increased if the performers have to attend to the audience as well as to their parts at the same time?

Can you not imagine how a play which has been rehearsed to perfection in dead silence without an audience must be upset, disjointed, and spun out to a wearisome length by an audience which refuses to enjoy it silently?

Have you noticed that if you laugh loudly and repeatedly for two hours, you get tired and cross, and are sorry next morning that you did not stay at home?

Will you think me very ungrateful and unkind if I tell you that though you cannot possibly applaud my plays too much at each fall of the curtain to please me, yet the more applause there is during the performance the angrier I feel with you for spoiling your enjoyment and my own?

Would you dream of stopping the performance of a piece of music to applaud every bar that happened to please you? and do you not know that an act of a play is intended, just like a piece of music, to be heard without interruption from beginning to end?

Have you ever told your sons and daughters that little children should be seen and not heard? And have you ever thought how nice theatrical performances would be, and how much sooner you would get away to supper, if parents in the theatre would follow the precepts they give to their children at home?

Have you noticed that people look very nice when they smile or look pleased, but look shockingly ugly when they roar with laughter or shout excitedly or sob loudly? Smiles make no noise.

Do you know that what pleases actors and authors most is not your applauding them but your coming to see the play again and again, and that if you tire yourselves out and spoil the play with interruptions you are very unlikely to come again?

Do you know that my plays, as rehearsed, are just the right length: that is, quite as long as you can bear; and that if you delay the performances by loud laughter you will make them half an hour too long?

Can I persuade you to let the performance proceed in perfect silence just this once to see how you like it. The intervals will give you no less than five opportunities of expressing your approval or disapproval, as the case may be.

And finally, will you believe me to be acting sincerely in your own interests in this matter as

your faithful servant,

THE AUTHOR.

New Year, 1913

Author's Note

(From the programme of the production at the
Regent Theatre, London, 15 February 1926)

John Bull's Other Island was written in 1904, when the Irish Free State
was unborn and undreamt of, and when Liberals like Mr Thomas Broadbent, still smarting from their recent unpopularity as pro-Boers, were
ardent advocates of Home Rule for Ireland, the emancipation of
Macedonia from the Turkish yoke, and, generally, an implacable resistance to oppression everywhere except at home. They believed that freedom would come to Ireland from the Gladstonian tradition; and if an
enchanter had shown them in a magic mirror the Easter rebellion, the
ruins of bombarded Dublin, the sanguinary campaign in which the Black-
and-Tans and Sinn Fein tried which could burn most houses until
Michael Collins won, and the armistice which established the Irish Free
State only to inaugurate a purely Irish civil war in which every bridge
in Ireland was broken, they would have regarded that enchanter as the
most ridiculous romancer that ever showed the grossest ignorance of the
modern, sensible, matter-of-fact, parliamentary world he was living in.
As to these events passing almost unnoticed in England because England
was fighting hard for her own life, and Broadbent's and several other
London houses had been blown to bits by the bombs of a foreign enemy,
that would have seemed too silly to be even funny.

The play you are about to see takes you back to that state of innocence
and false security. As no attempt has been made to bring it up to date,
the younger members of the audience must listen as patiently as they
can to Mr Broadbent delivering a few speeches which will make them
wonder what on earth he is talking about. But, in the main, human nature,
though it has changed its catchwords a little, is very much what it was
then. There are still Rosscullens in Ireland and still Broadbents in
England. I do not believe there is a single character in the play that you
may not find today not perceptibly different from what he or she was
then. The Macdona Players therefore present the play just as it was,
feeling confident that its few discrepancies with the world just as it is

will not prevent you from enjoying it, and may even add to your amusement.

G. B. S.

MORE ABOUT PENGUINS, PELICANS AND PUFFINS

For further information about books available from Penguins please write to Dept EP, Penguin Books Ltd, Harmondsworth, Middlesex UB7 0DA.

In the U.S.A.: For a complete list of books available from Penguins in the United States write to Dept DG, Penguin Books, 299 Murray Hill Parkway, East Rutherford, New Jersey 07073.

In Canada: For a complete list of books available from Penguins in Canada write to Penguin Books Canada Ltd, 2801 John Street, Markham, Ontario L3R 1B4.

In Australia: For a complete list of books available from Penguins in Australia write to the Marketing Department, Penguin Books Australia Ltd, P.O. Box 257, Ringwood, Victoria 3134.

In New Zealand: For a complete list of books available from Penguins in New Zealand write to the Marketing Department, Penguin Books (N.Z.) Ltd, P.O. Box 4019, Auckland 10.

In India: For a complete list of books available from Penguins in India write to Penguin Overseas Ltd, 706 Eros Apartments, 56 Nehru Place, New Delhi 110019.

THE PENGUIN SHAW

Bernard Shaw's *The Intelligent Woman's Guide to Socialism, Capitalism, Sovietism, and Fascism* was the first Pelican book to be published, in May 1937. Since then many of his plays have been published as Penguins. All of them are complete with Shaw's original prefaces, which put the argument of his play in strong and witty terms and serve as examples of Shaw's individual and assertive prose style. The following are published:

GEORGE BERNARD SHAW

THE BLACK GIRL IN SEARCH OF GOD
AND SOME LESSER TALES

The centrepiece of this colourful collection is *The Black Girl in Search of God*, a tale in the manner of Voltaire's *Candide*. In her search for the true God, the black girl encounters a series of old gentlemen, generally clothed in long white nightshirts. When she is tired of arguing and of laying about her with her knobkerry, she settles down with a redhaired Irish socialist, following Voltaire's advice that the wisest attitude to life is to cultivate one's own garden.

The *Lesser Tales* range from a satirical fairy story featuring a charwoman's entry into heaven, to an obituary of an old revolutionary hero; from an essay (in dramatic form) on the theatre, to an exposition of Don Giovanni's character. All these tales bear the true Shavian imprint; some unashamedly pack a message, others satirize outworn ideas and institutions. All are confident and incisive.

CASHEL BYRON'S PROFESSION

Bernard Shaw was obsessed with prize-fighting all his life – he entered the English Amateur Boxing Association Championship as middleweight – and his racy, romantic, adventure story superbly evokes the bruised knuckles and raw hopes of the ringside.

After pole-axing his mathematics master with a perfect right, Cashel Byron, the unloved son of a successful actress, runs away to Australia. He returns, and becomes the most famous fighter of his age, only to be floored by the lovely and impossible Lydia Carew.

'Genuine and remarkable narrative talent ... a talent of strength, spirit, capacity ... it is all mad, mad and deliriously delightful ... All I ask is more of it' – Robert Louis Stevenson.

Also published:

THE INTELLIGENT WOMAN'S GUIDE TO
SOCIALISM, CAPITALISM, SOVIETISM AND FASCISM

DAVID STOREY IN PENGUIN PLAYS

Home/The Changing Room/Mother's Day

HOME

'As a view of crippled lives and wintry tenderness between them, the play is beautifully spare and sustained in tone' – Ronald Bryden in the *Observer*.

THE CHANGING ROOM

Behind the ribbing, and the swearing, and the showing off, the piece is permeated by a Wordsworthian spirit. You can, if you listen, hear through it "the still, sad music of humanity"' – Harold Hobson in the *Sunday Times*.

MOTHER'S DAY

'Mr Storey's farcical invention is tireless, and has the advantage of unlimited permissiveness' – *Financial Times*.

Early Days/Sisters/Life Class

EARLY DAYS

'It has the insidious simplicity of a piano piece by Satie or a Wordsworth lyrical ballad ... it touches deep chords' – Michael Billington in the *Guardian*.

SISTERS

'Deals in betrayal, love and finally, madness ... a remarkable, stimulating, and unsettling gem of a play' – Gerard Dempsey in the *Daily Express*.

LIFE CLASS

'Art itself may have moved into happenings some years ago; but, to my knowledge, this is the stage's first tribute of that event, and we are not likely to see it bettered' – Irving Wardle in *The Times*.

ALSO PUBLISHED IN PENGUIN PLAYS

A VOYAGE ROUND MY FATHER
AND OTHER PLAYS

John Mortimer

'John Mortimer's funny, subtle, touching portrait. It is his father's enigmatic endurance that concerns him and enriches us' – J. W. Lambert in the *Sunday Times*.

'There is hardly a line in these plays which does not create a vivid picture in the hearer's mind, and stir his memory, and disturb his imagination, and fill it with vague, impalpable feelings of remembered disappointments and delights' – Harold Hobson in the *Sunday Times*.

LA RONDE

Arthur Schnitzler

Adapted by John Barton for the Royal Shakespeare Company.

Written over eighty years ago, this extraordinary play provoked anti-semitic riots in Berlin and uproar in Vienna. After a subsequent obscenity trial, the author banned any performances of *La Ronde* in Europe until after his death.

Sharp, sophisticated and coolly savage, it is a brilliant exposé of human sexuality which was far ahead of its time. Set in turn-of-the-century Vienna, it depicts ten characters – all linked in a sexual chain – who together explore the whole spectrum of sexual response.

THE LITTLE FOXES/ANOTHER PART OF THE FOREST

Lilian Hellman

The Little Foxes Set in the American Deep South in 1900, this is a searing drama of bitter conflict within the family and of the hatred and greed that is slowly destroying the old loyalties that had once united them.

Another Part of the Forest Twenty years earlier, the same family are seen in Alabama when the seeds of their future discord are sown.

ALSO PUBLISHED IN PENGUIN PLAYS

PARABLES FOR THE THEATRE

Bertolt Brecht

The Good Women of Setzuan and *The Caucasian Chalk Circle* are among the handful of plays generally regarded as the master-pieces of one of the dominating figures in the modern theatre. Both plays are well-known from productions in this country, and *The Caucasian Chalk Circle* in particular is an outstanding example of Brecht's epic theatre. The versions in this edition are those of Eric Bentley, a close friend of Brecht's and for many years one of the most energetic advocates of his work.

ABSURD DRAMA

Eugène Ionesco/AMÉDÉE OR HOW TO GET RID OF IT
Arthur Adamov/PROFESSOR TARANNE
Fernando Arrabal/THE TWO EXECUTIONERS
Edward Albee/THE ZOO STORY

'It aims to shock its audience out of complacency, to bring it face to face with the harsh facts of the human situation as these writers see it. But ... in the last resort, the Theatre of the Absurd does not provoke tears of despair but the laughter of liberation' – from the introduction by Martin Esslin.

FOUR PLAYS

Günter Grass

Flood and *Onkel, Onkel* can be seen as fables of post-war Germany; *Only Ten Minutes to Buffalo* mocks the stationary driver who thinks he is advancing at top speed; and *The Wicked Cooks* is an exuberant allegory which the *Observer* called 'false fantasy, mock history, a scaring, comic and thoroughly political play, a kind of trick with echoes'.

'He is a good painter, an excellent poet. He is the most famous novelist in modern Germany, and deserves to be so. He is a brilliant, alarmingly acrobatic playwright' – *Observer*.

ALSO PUBLISHED IN PENGUIN PLAYS

CLASSIC IRISH DRAMA

Introduced by W. A. Armstrong

Yeats's *The Countess Cathleen* tells of two merchants who traffic in men's souls, and of how the Countess sells her own rather than see her people starve.

Synge's *The Playboy of the Western World* is about a peasant boy who thinks he has killed his father and so becomes a hero – until his murdered father reappears.

O'Casey's *Cock-a-doodle Dandy*, which the author considered his best play, is a satire directed against superstition, avarice and priestly authority.

THE GOLDEN AGE OF SOVIET THEATRE

Introduced and Edited by Michael Glenny

The Bedbug 'One of the most devastating satires of Communist society in contemporary literature' – Patricia Blake.

Marya 'Babel sets out to record the truth and the complexity of social change, to capture the instant when one era ended and another began' – Michael Glenny

The Dragon One of 'the most penetrating and certainly the funniest studies ever made of tyranny and the moral corruption of both tyrants and subjects' – Michael Glenny.

THREE EUROPEAN PLAYS

Introduced and Edited by E. Martin Browne

In his ebullient comedy, *Ring Round the Moon*, Anouilh draws vivid and entertaining portraits of human idiosyncrasies – with a total disregard for accepted moral value. Ugo Betti's reputation now rivals that of Pirandello; his concern with morality and religion is demonstrated in *The Queen and the Rebels*, a political drama of our own times written in the classical tradition. Sartre's *In Camera* involves three of life's victims who come to recognize that 'hell is other people'.